WILDLIFE
GUARDIAN

WILDLIFE GUARDIAN
Stories of a Pennsylvania Game Warden

By

William Wasserman

ISBN 978-0-9718907-1-8

Cover by Timothy Flanigan

IV

ALSO BY WILLIAM WASSERMAN

Game Warden: *Adventures of a Wildlife Warrior*

Poacher Wars: *A Pennsylvania Game Warden's Journal*

Pennsylvania Wildlife Tails*: A Game Warden's Notebook*

More Pennsylvania Wildlife Tails: *A Game Warden's Notebook II*

Dedication

Photo by Bill Schwartz-Gettysburg Times

Pennsylvania Game Commission Wildlife Conservation Officer David L. Grove was shot and killed in the line of duty on November 11, 2010 while attempting to arrest a deer poacher.

A graduate of the 27th class of the Game Commission's Ross Leffler School of Conservation, Grove was assigned to Adams County as a full time Wildlife Conservation Officer on March 8, 2008.

David Grove was a bright, young officer who loved hunting, fishing, and the great outdoors. He dedicated his life to our natural resources and wildlife conservation.

While alone on night patrol, in an area where poaching activity had been reported, this courageous wildlife guardian made the ultimate sacrifice in the performance of his duty. It is to him for whom I dedicate this book.

Introduction

While it is true that some poachers kill wildlife for subsistence, most incidents are perpetrated by outlaws with criminal histories who kill countless birds and animals with no intention of retrieving a single carcass. For them, poaching is about target practice, not survival. After a night's shoot, I might find a dozen or more carcasses lying in open fields.

Others shoot deer solely for their antlers. They leave the carcasses to be picked apart by coyotes and other scavengers. These are practiced butchers who can jump from a vehicle and skull-cap a buck in seconds. More than a few will be once-in-a-lifetime racks—trophy deer that the honest hunter never gets to see in the wild. But for the poacher, they are fond mementos. Illicit kills that only a warped mind can appreciate.

Having spent more than half my life tracking down and arresting outlaw hunters, I've encountered all kinds. This book contains stories about some of these people. I like to think of it as the good, the bad, and the ugly of the poachers' universe.

The incidents recounted in this book are real; however, the stories are based on my memories over a period of years and may differ from the memories of others. I admit to taking some creative liberties with events and to re-creating some of the dialog. I have also given the poachers and their associates fictitious names and have altered their physical descriptions. Any resemblance to actual persons, living or dead, is entirely coincidental.

What would the world be,
once bereft of wet and wildness?
O let them be left, wildness and wet.
Long live the weeds and the wilderness yet.
— Gerard Manley Hopkins

I have got you out here in the great open spaces
where cats are cats.

~Don Marquis

Footsteps in the Dark

To SAY I WAS IRKED when the complaint about a marauding cougar came crackling through the speakers of my Chevy Blazer would be an understatement. After all, I expected the same tiresome outcome that every other cougar complaint had brought me over the years.

A short time later, alone in the bleak, uncompromising night, I realized that I couldn't have been more wrong . . .

Oh please, not now! It was deer season, with poaching activity at its peak. The last thing I needed was to waste time on some wild goose—er, cougar chase.

I picked up my mike and asked dispatch to repeat the message, hoping against hope that I'd heard it wrong.

"We have a complaint that a *couuugar* just killed a goat," the voice crackled back, purposely drawing out the word for me. "It's at the Lewis property in Dark Hollow. They're requesting an officer respond immediately."

Deputy Joe Wenzel and I exchanged glances of open skepticism. "Cougar?" he said. Although assigned to me as a cadet fresh from the Training School, he'd been a deputy game warden for over a decade before attending the academy and had plenty of hands-on experience.

"Cougar, mountain lion, puma—must have checked a hundred supposed sightings in the last twenty years," I told him. "Not one of them ever panned out." I pulled into a side road to turn around and keyed the mike. "Ten-four, we're in route."

Wenzel watched through the windshield, the full moon playing across his face as an ebony landscape raced by. "They call them mountain lions out my way," he said. "People claim they're seeing them all the time—big cats that weigh over a hundred pounds. I don't know what they're *really* seeing. I've never found any evidence that mountain lions live around here."

"Bobcats mostly," I suggested. "A big one will go thirty-five pounds and look like it weighs seventy, especially if it's out in the open with nothing to compare it to. Dogs, bears, coyotes, fishers—you name it. I've had them all mistaken for big cats over the years. Deer too."

Wenzel looked surprised. "Deer?"

"Last year I got a call about a road killed cougar that turned out to be a doe," I said. "Both animals have similar colored coats, depending on the time of year. The deer was lying on the berm with a broken hind leg pointing straight out behind it like a long tail. Its black hoof convinced the motorist all the more that he'd seen a dead cougar, right down to the black tip on its tail."

"No wonder we get so many mountain lion reports if people are mistaking deer for them."

"The news media doesn't help either. They love to perpetuate the myth—sensationalize it. I've seen newspaper articles and TV programs show footage of housecats that were supposedly cougars. Somebody calls and claims they saw one—the press runs with it. Anything to sell a story."

Wenzel frowned. "Makes it tough to believe us when we say they aren't here."

"Sure does. Thing is, we used to have a lot of cougars in Pennsylvania. The Commonwealth even paid a bounty on them once: eight bucks a head back in the eighteen hundreds. Good money considering that the average worker made about sixteen dollars a week. As a result, they were wiped out. The last one was killed over a hundred years ago."

"What about escaped cougars? A zoo, traveling circus—something like that? Think one might be out there somewhere?"

"It's definitely possible. Unlikely. But possible."

"So this could be the real thing, huh?"

"Yeah. Could be. Nervous?"

"More like excited. You?"

"Morbid curiosity," I said. "Waiting for the day it actually comes true. And hoping it never does. It's not that I don't think a cougar could exist here; it's just that a confirmed cougar sighting would make too many people think we have a viable population. The rumors are bad enough already. There are people who actually believe the Game Commission has secretly reintroduced cougars into the state to help control the deer herd. They're absolutely convinced! I once had a woman tell me that her husband saw a truckload of cougars with a Game Commission decal on it parked along a back road in Bradford County. Looked me right in the eye, too. Daring me to deny it."

"What did you tell her?"

"Nothing. I walked away. Wondered what else her husband was lying to her about."

Wenzel shook his head. "Yeah. Really."

"People believe what they want to believe. It's frustrating. The last authentic eastern cougar was killed in Maine back in 1938. Some trapper from up in Canada got him."

"What about Florida? They have a cougar population; the Florida panther is their state animal."

"Yes, and it's the only known breeding population of cougars east of the Mississippi River. Which brings up a good point: occasionally Florida has one killed on the highway. We never do. And with a million hunters roaming the woods in deer season, you'd think we'd have a cougar killed every so often. Mistaken for a deer, shot for a trophy—something!"

"How about an actual track or a scat?" added Wenzel. "You'd think somebody would have found one we could confirm by now; or maybe some blood or hair that could be analyzed."

"Yes. Something real. Instead of all the phony photographs floating around the Internet. I saw another one last week. The caption said, *'Here's a picture of a cougar on my patio in Wyoming County. It was watching my kids on the kitchen floor.'* Turns out the photograph was actually taken in Colorado!"

"I saw it too. Only it claimed the cabin was in Sullivan County. Lord knows how many patios that cougar visited over the years," Wenzel said with a dry chuckle.

"How about black panthers? Get any of those? I've been hearing about them for the last thirty years. A guy claiming to be a state biologist once told me two cougars crossed right in front of him when he was hiking along the Appalachian Trail. Said they stopped to look him over for a minute before moving on. Said one was brown, the other was black. I don't know what he saw, but there has never been a black cougar captured, killed or confirmed anywhere in the world. Not ever. They simply don't exist. Leopards and jaguars are known to have a melanistic phase, but not cougars."

16

"Did you tell him?"

"I did."

"And he said . . ."

"Might as well have told him the moon was made of cheese. He saw what he saw. Period. For all I know he was looking at two Labrador retrievers—but they definitely weren't cougars."

A red fox darted across my path, its coat long and silky. I took my foot off the gas to avoid hitting it. Wildlife seemed particularly active tonight. It was late autumn, winter close at hand.

"We're almost there," I said.

I could feel Wenzel's eyes boring into me as I focused on the highway ahead. "So, you've never had a cougar sighting that you thought was authentic, is that what you're saying?"

"Actually, there was this one time . . ."

He waited for me to continue.

"Gonna tell me about it or keep it to yourself?"

I glanced at him and shrugged. "I was stationed in Montgomery County, not far from Philadelphia, when I got this report of a big cat. There were too many coincidental sightings to believe it was anything else. It's the only time I investigated a cougar sighting that I thought might be authentic.

"The local police chief came to my house and asked if I wanted to go on a safari—his words, 'a safari.' He was dead serious. Said he and his deputy saw a mountain lion jump across a jeep trail right in front of them. They were in an open field behind a housing development, investigating a nine-one-one call about a tiger that a woman claimed she saw in her back yard. It was a legitimate call, according to the chief. Except he swore it was a mountain lion, not a tiger. Said he'd seen them before while on hunting trips out west."

"Big difference," remarked Wenzel.

"Yeah, that's what I thought. One has stripes, one doesn't. I accompanied the chief back to the field where he saw the cat. Looked everywhere. No tracks of course. We hadn't had rain in weeks. No cat either. Whatever it was, was long gone.

So I interviewed the woman who originally called in the complaint. Nice lady: housewife, mid-thirties, intelligent. Said she looked out her window and saw a tiger rolling on its back in the grass! I asked if she was absolutely certain. She asked what other cat weighs over a hundred pounds and has black stripes.

"Afterwards I got phone calls every day for the next two weeks. Some people claimed they saw a cougar, others called to say they heard catlike screams at night. Folks were nervous. Can't say that I blame them, either. In the end, nobody got any photographs, and I never found so much as a single track. But I believe there was some kind of wild cat moving through the county. The incident never made the news, so there was no reason for anyone to anticipate, or even imagine, that a big cat might be lurking in their neighborhood. None of the complainants knew each other either. Thing is, as time went by, the complaints tracked progressively northward, indicating the cat traveled about fifteen miles per day until it left the county."

"What do you think it was?"

"I figured it had to be some kind of wild cat, most likely someone's pet. The first sighting was close to the Philadelphia line. Three million people lived within a fifty-mile radius of the place. Any one of them could have purchased an exotic cat somewhere, found out they couldn't keep it any longer and decided to release it into the wild. Or it could've just slipped its cage one day, who knows. The thing that had me baffled, though, was the stripes. The tiger lady and the police chief both saw the same animal. Didn't make sense—or so I thought, until I picked up a book depicting wild cats of the world and came up with the only logical answer: an ocelot."

"Heard of them. Endangered, right?"

"Yes. There's a tiny population down in Texas and Arizona—less than fifty. They're found mostly in South America now. And get this: the cat got its name from the Aztec Indians in Mexico; it means field tiger. A large ocelot can weigh over forty pounds and measure five feet long from nose to tail, which would make it look eighty or even a hundred pounds to the untrained eye. Their reddish brown coats are covered with black spots and rosettes that cluster into what looks like irregular stripes or bands, similar to a tiger. They have definite black stripes on their face and neck too. I think the lady who saw the cat in her back yard got a close look at the animal and saw what she thought were stripes on a tiger. The police chief, on the other hand, merely caught a glimpse of the cat as it leaped across the trail in front of him, its pelt a blur, which made it look like a mountain lion."

I turned on my left blinker and nudged the break. "We're here."

A rural community of perhaps five hundred people, Dark Hollow lies between two mountain peaks in extreme northwestern Wyoming County. It consists of a single church, a convenience store boasting two gas pumps, and a small diner famous for its home baked pies and cakes. The village is split in half by a two-lane macadam state road that wends its way into the adjacent Endless Mountains, known for some of the finest hunting and fishing in the Commonwealth.

The folks who live there are hard working, God fearing, gun toting individualists. And they are clannish, especially when it comes to law enforcement.

Although I'd been working in Wyoming County for many years, this was the first time a resident of Dark Hollow had ever asked to see a game warden. The mountains surrounding the community were part of my regular patrol during big game season; I'd often pass through Dark Hollow on my way into them. Sadly, it was the only village in my four-hundred-square-mile district that I could be certain no one would wave a friendly "hello" as I drove by. On the positive side, I didn't receive any other hand gestures either.

The folks here may not have welcomed me, but they respected me nevertheless.

Poaching was a common occurrence in Dark Hollow. Most folks accepted it as a way of life. Wild critters were here for the taking, so long as you ate the meat and didn't kill indiscriminately. This was the evolved law these mountain folk embraced. It's how they were brought up. If you lived by the code, everything would be fine and dandy. Choose to disregard it, the consequences could get ugly. Vigilante justice, as some had learned, can be extremely unforgiving.

I'd made a number of arrests here over the years, most were relatively minor in nature: an occasional untagged deer, loaded guns in vehicles, road hunting—incidents that I'd encountered by chance, while on routine patrol. Because game wardens generally have a huge area to cover—in my case the entire county—the odds of stumbling upon a big case were as remote as the very mountains that surrounded me. Game wardens, like all police officers, typically get their best cases through informants. People living in rural communities know what goes on around them. Gossip is as common as the sunrise. Often, all it takes in an anonymous tip, a single phone call, to set the stage for a major poaching bust. But inside information coming from Dark Hollow was about as likely as snow in July.

Still, because I had blundered into some illegal activity here over the years, I'd managed to develop a reputation, which brought me a certain respect among not only the law-abiding citizens but many of the outlaw clans operating in my district as well. I was glad for it. Being a game warden in rural America places you constantly under a microscope. You're often regarded as somewhat of a celebrity; consequently, your reputation, good or bad, is gained at breakneck speed—sometimes in a matter of days.

As I eased my Blazer down the long, dirt driveway leading to the Lewis residence, a man and a woman stood on the covered porch, necks craning to see my marked vehicle looming toward them in the dark. The house, a two-story, wood framed country home, its exterior sided with gray weathered shingles, looked to be fifty years old or so, as were most homes scattered about the hollow.

Coal smoke drifted lazily from the chimney, giving the chilly air a sulphur-like smell that reminded me of gunpowder as Wenzel and I exited my vehicle and stepped up on the porch.

"Glad you could come," the man said grimly. He wrapped an arm around the woman and pulled her close, as if protecting her. "I'm Zach Lewis. This is my wife, Millie."

Both were in their seventies. He of medium height and skinny as a fencepost. He wore tan chinos with a quilted, blue plaid shirt. A red Phillies baseball cap had been pulled all the way to his ears, causing the tips to curl down like wilted flowers. Mrs. Lewis, shorter than her husband but outweighing him considerably, wore a denim skirt and heavy woolen sweater. Her jowly face was soft and pleasant with round-rimmed glasses and a perpetual smile. She reminded me of someone who might play Mrs. Santa Claus in a Disney movie.

"State Game Commission," I said. "You called about a cougar?"

"Yessir," said Zach Lewis. His eyebrows jiggled fiercely at the mere mention of the beast. "It killed my goat!"

"Poor Scooter," sighed Mrs. Lewis. "He was like part of our family."

"What makes you think it was a cougar?" I asked.

"We've been hearing them scream at night for weeks!" declared Zach Lewis. "It's the most bloodcurdling sound I ever heard."

"Sure it's not bobcats? They make an awful cry."

His lips drew into a deep frown. "I knew you wouldn't believe me! Ain't that right, Millie? I told you they wouldn't believe me, didn't I."

Mrs. Lewis nodded in agreement, her face turning grave.

"My brother saw one just yesterday!" he declared. "A huge yellow cat with a long tail. Oh, they're here all right."

"It's not that I don't believe you, sir. It's just that cougars haven't lived in Pennsylvania for over a hundred years; lots of people mistake bobcats for them."

"Pooh! That's what you want us to believe; they've been in these hills for years. Why, I hear the Game Commission brought them into the state from out west to thin the deer herd—that you're in cahoots with the insurance companies. Too many deer hit by cars." He squeezed his wife's shoulder for support. "Must be working too. Not seeing the deer like we used to."

"We hardly see them any more," parroted Millie. "Beautiful creatures."

"Think poaching might have something to do with that?" I said.

The old man's eyes narrowed into slits. "Folks here might jacklight a deer once in a while, but it's to put meat on the table. It's not like we're market hunters, wiping out the herd or anything like that."

"It's still against the law," I said, realizing at once that my words were in vain.

"Law's not always right!" barked Lewis, his face brittle with rage. "Besides, some pencil pusher in Harrisburg ain't telling me or my family how we should live! This is *our* land. We take care of our own."

Why do I do this to myself?

"It's getting late, sir," I said, changing the subject. "I think it's time we take a look at that goat."

The old man cocked his head and looked at me as if he'd suddenly remembered why we were here. His face slowly softening, he shook his head with sorrow. "Scooter's up there," he said, pointing a crooked finger into the night. "Just follow the footpath into the woods and you'll come to him.

Go on," he insisted, motioning us forward. "I'll be right behind you."

We walked through a field of grass tinged in bright silver moonlight until we came to a perimeter of trees fifty yards away. This was no tiny woodlot. Here the forest stretched uninterrupted for a hundred miles north and west. We were on the edge of some of the wildest country in the state, and I supposed a cougar or just about any other animal could roam here undetected for a lifetime if it wanted. The still night was unusual for November when north winds are prevalent, and I couldn't help but listen for shots in the distance as we pushed ahead. With any luck, Wenzel and I would fall into a poaching incident while we were here. The trip worthwhile after all—

"Do you have a holster for that cannon?" barked Wenzel.

I spun around to look into the deadly muzzle of a .44 Magnum revolver! My stomach roiled when I saw the hammer cocked. Zach Lewis had been trailing me with his gun pointed absently at my back the entire time.

He lowered the muzzle. His face a blank stare.

"You trying to kill somebody?" I growled.

"Just trying to protect myself!" hissed Lewis, eyebrows jiggling crazily. "You gotta be ready. They hide up in the trees, you know—jump down and ambush you!"

I turned to Wenzel. His expression sheer wonderment. Until that moment, we hadn't even realized Lewis was armed. "Holster it or leave now," I said.

The old man considered his options for a moment, his face a scowl of discontent. Reluctantly he opened his quilted shirt and stuffed the heavy gun into his belt. "Just don't blame me if the cougar gets you before I can put a bullet in it!" he grumbled.

"Don't worry; I won't. Promise."

Bathed in the warm glow of my five-cell Kel-lite, a goat lay dead. Its neck snapped like a matchstick. Chained to a medium-sized oak, there had been no chance of escape. The doomed creature had run in a panic-stricken circle, its twenty-foot leash wrapping tighter and tighter around the tree until it became bound hopelessly to its trunk. Mouth agape as if crying out, its delicate white belly had been ripped open, grey intestines coiled on the ground like a dozing python.

"Poor Scooter," muttered Zach Lewis, his voice broken. "He didn't deserve to die like this."

I scanned the terrain with my flashlight, hoping to find a track or scat left behind, but there was nothing. It had to be something big, I thought. Something with tremendous jaw strength. Whatever killed the goat had bitten clean through its neck, severing the spinal cord.

Suddenly, the thick penetrating groan of a large animal came from the woods behind us.

We froze.

"That's no bobcat!" I said.

Wenzel's eyes cut toward the sound. He nodded in agreement.

At the Philadelphia Zoo, just a week ago with my family, I'd heard the African lions roaring at feeding time. Actually, it wasn't so much a roar as a low, guttural moaning followed by a series of deep, grunting huffs. A wild and ferocious sound. An unforgettable sound.

Much like the one I just heard.

Again it came, perhaps twenty yards off, a deep and hungry moan that seemed to roll through the night into your very soul.

I looked at Wenzel, my scalp tightening. He cocked his head and shrugged, indicating he didn't know what to make of it.

"Excuse me," said Lewis, eyebrows jumping frantically under his cap. "I think I'll retreat now."

I didn't blame him a bit, and welcomed his departure. The last thing I needed was Zach Lewis taking wild potshots at the dark.

"No problem," I said. "You be careful going back."

Legs pumping like jackhammers, he fled down the footpath toward home. "Better arm yourselves with something besides your six-shooters!" he hollered without looking back. "Might not be enough to knock down a big cat!"

Wenzel and I both had state-issued, Smith and Wesson .357 Magnum revolvers holstered on our belts. Between us, we could do a lot of damage. But shooting at a moving target in the dark can be challenging at best. Lewis was right: we needed something that would stop whatever came at us with one shot.

A dead branch cracked like a two-by-four.

Something heavy slid through the laurels to our right, its body scraping the brush as it maneuvered closer.

"Whatever's out there really wants that goat," said Wenzel.

"Or us," I cautioned.

I told him about the lions at the zoo. His face hardened with concern. "Maybe one escaped from that menagerie in New York; it's less than a hundred miles from here," he said. "They have lions, tigers, and other big cats over there."

"That's what I'm thinking too."

"What do you want to do?"

"Wait here until it comes for the goat."

Wenzel palmed the butt of his sidearm, eyes scanning the trees for movement. "Knew you were gonna say that."

Better arm yourselves with something besides your six-shooters. Might not be enough to knock down a big cat . . .

"One more thing," I said, handing him my flashlight. "I want you to go back to the Blazer and get my twelve-gauge. Magazine's loaded with double-aught buck, but I have rifled slugs in the glove box. Dump the buckshot, load it with slugs, and bring it back here."

Wenzel smiled. "Knew you were gonna say that too."

25

As I stood within the vast darkness surrounding me, the creature began to move, coming gradually closer until I could hear the steady cadence of its panting.

I drew my .357 revolver, knowing that it wouldn't be enough to stop a truly large animal unless my aim was dead on—unlikely, under the circumstances. Although I could tell roughly where the creature had positioned itself, I didn't want to make a sound-shot and risk wounding it. It might make the situation worse. Besides, I really didn't know what was lurking out there, and refused to shoot at something I couldn't see, even if it meant risking my own welfare.

The panting ceased.

A sudden silence now.

I dropped to one knee. Gripping my revolver in two hands, combat style, I braced myself in the direction the animal might come from if it attacked. I remained stock-still, eyes searching the abyss, ears straining to detect the slightest movement. Unlike humans, most animals can see quite well at night. Some, like cats, hunt primarily with their eyes.

I wondered if it was sizing me up at this very moment, its powerful body adjusting, muscles taut and ready. The notion made my heart hammer so loud I could actually hear it.

And I was certain whatever was out there could too.

Suddenly there came a terrible roar as a huge shadow sprang from the trees, its awful weight crushing me. Knife-like claws tore into my chest, shredding my coat like tissue paper. I shoved my knees into its belly, attempting to push the beast off. Instead, something wet and warm began to collect under my back, soaking it. I realized with horror that it was my own blood. I cried out as its brutal jaws clamped on the back of my neck. My gun! I dropped my gun...!

I shook the nightmare out of my skull. A lifetime working around wild animals, including aggressive bears, had never caused me so much as a scratch, and I wasn't about to let that change tonight. I closed my eyes and took a deep breath. Exhaling ever so slowly, I cocked my good ear toward the woods and listened.

Quiet as a cemetery, it seemed I would hear a leaf falling to the ground as I kept my handgun ready. Then, as if sensing my intent, the beast began to slowly withdraw, moving deeper into the woods, perhaps fifty yards or so before pausing. A wave of relief washed over me as I lowered the revolver's muzzle.

Letting out a long breath, I looked toward heaven and smiled. It was as if God had taken a brush and painted the universe with a billion diamonds—more stars than I had ever seen before, so it seemed tonight. They sparkled and danced for me as I gazed at them, and I wondered in awe at how a night could be so beautiful and yet so grim.

"Come onnn, Joe," I whispered anxiously.

T he dead goat smelled terrible. Like what, I didn't know—stinky feet? vomit? a combination of the two? Offensive as it was, something about the odor proved vaguely familiar. I sniffed gingerly at the air. What was it? Then, suddenly, it came to me: limburger cheese! When I was a kid, (no pun intended) my father would have it occasionally for an afternoon snack. The appalling smell drove everyone—my mother, brother, sister, and me—out of the kitchen and into another room at the mere opening of a package. I remembered him sitting at the table, all by himself, happily sawing through a yellow brick of the stuff with a sharp knife. Sometimes he'd catch me as I passed by. *Sure you don't want some?* he'd offer cheerily. I'd wrinkle my nose. *Yuk, Dad! It stinks!* He'd let out a good-natured laugh. *Try it, it's good! The smell goes away as soon as you start eating it.* Struck dumb at the jarring thought of tasting the funky cheese, I'd shake my head and dash off to seek safe refuge with the rest of my family.

As for ol' Scooter: if I could smell him, whatever was spooking around out there in the dark could too—and at a far greater intensity. No doubt, the goat's scorching odor had spawned a ravenous craving in its belly. Like they say: one man's meat is another man's poison. What stunk to me, apparently transformed into an alluring aroma for the creature lurking in the woods.

My brother saw one just yesterday . . . a huge yellow cat with a long tail.

Zach Lewis and his brother had been born and raised in Dark Hollow, where every child, boy or girl, has a gun in their hands by age seven. They had spent a lifetime hunting and tracking big game; and they were absolutely convinced that cougars inhabited the area and that one of these big cats had killed Zach's goat. Although any predator might attack its prey by the neck, I was painfully aware that it is a common trait of great cats, and I was becoming more convinced by the minute that they were right. Except that I envisioned a much larger cat.

Over the years, I'd come across more than a few people harboring exotic wildlife they'd purchased overseas. I once assisted with a case in Bucks County where a man kept a four-hundred-pound African lion in his barn. Pennsylvania statues require all exotic wildlife, especially big cats, to be locked in an adequate cage at all times; but this individual thought nothing of parading down busy Main Street with the lion in the open bed of his pickup truck. As if that wasn't bad enough, he'd often walk the cat on a leash like a dog, causing general alarm throughout the neighborhood he lived in. Game Warden Ed Bond and I had our hands full getting him to comply with the law. In truth, to this day, I don't know that we ever really did; we couldn't watch him round-the-clock. I often thought that one day we'd get a call that his lion had killed someone. Fortunately, we never did.

And if the thing in the woods was one of the great cats of the world, it would be back. Of this, I was certain.

Only next time it might not give up so easily.

By the time Wenzel returned, a thick cloud cover had made the night dark as an Egyptian tomb. I watched the winking glow of his light as he approached through the woods, relieved to see him.

"Anything happen while I was gone?" he asked, handing me the shotgun.

"It's still out there," I said. "Waiting to make its next move."

Wenzel hesitated, then whiffed at the air a moment. "What's that?

"It's the goat, Joe."

"Hmmm, smells like Limburger cheese."

"You say that like it's a *good* thing."

"It is if you like Limburger cheese."—

Something moved behind us. Something big. And it was coming fast!

We spun on our heels. I dropped to one knee, shotgun pointed toward the crashing sound. "Joe!" I hissed. "Wait till I give you the word, then turn on the flashlight!"

I thumbed the safety off and braced myself for a straight shot: right knee on the ground to support my weight, the other bent, securing my left elbow as I leaned into the shotgun. I expelled a long breath and waited. Wenzel stood behind me, ready to light up my target.

Come on and take your medicine . . . !

I'd seen what a twelve gauge rifled slug could do to human flesh in hunting accidents. Autopsies can be particularly grisly after someone is hit by one of these missiles; hence, I had no doubt that a single headshot would drop the creature in its tracks. But what I didn't know was whether I'd have a chance to make the shot before the thing was on top of me.

Wenzel and I scarcely breathed. Unlike before, I heard no hesitation in its approach. Instead, it moved purposefully through the trees, smashing small saplings in its path, coming closer with each passing second, a thick and steady huffing in its throat.

My heart galloped. My breathing thickened. And worse, I felt a whopper of a headache coming on. Oh, how I hated them!

All at once, as if an invisible curtain dropped from the sky, everything stopped. A thousand ants crawled up and down my back. The woods eerily quiet as I stared into the yawning darkness, eyes wide and searching. I listened with strained ears but heard only my pulse pounding in my brain.

Where is it . . . ?

Then, like fog rising from the earth, a large and indistinct shape appeared in front of me.

"Now!" I cried.

Wenzel's beam shot like a laser over my right shoulder, hitting the creature square in the face.

It blinked and shook its heavy head, temporarily dazed by the light.

Astonished, I took to my feet. It must have weighed five hundred pounds! A mere ten yards away, it stood its ground, examining me cautiously.

Then it took a step.

I adjusted my aim and squeezed the trigger. The twelve-gauge roared like a cannon, spewing a jagged yellow flame into the night, its deadly projectile boring harmlessly into a tree stump. The creature, frightened but unscathed, turned to disappear into the forest in a steady, lumbering gait.

I looked at Wenzel and shook my head. "I can't believe it!"

Wenzel gazed in the direction it had run, listening to it crash through the distant woods. "I don't know where it's headed but I sure hope it ends up someplace far away—someplace where there are no goats to kill, too."

"Or game wardens to terrorize," I added. "I think I just lost a year out of my life."

As we traveled along the state highway on our way through Dark Hollow, I noticed Wenzel staring wistfully out the windshield.

"What's on your mind?" I asked.

"The news didn't go over too well with Mr. Lewis, did it?"

"That's for sure. After hearing my shotgun go off, he's more convinced than ever that it was a cougar."

"I can't believe he thinks we'd lie about it—that we'd gut-shoot a cougar so it would run off someplace and die, just so we could say it was a bear. What makes him so suspicious of us, anyway?"

"It's not just us, Joe. It's *all* government employees—local, state or federal. Folks in Dark Hollow like to keep to themselves—govern themselves. It's a way of life for them. Besides, his brother claims he saw a cougar just yesterday; who's he going to believe, him or us?"

Wenzel grew quite for a moment. "I guess we really can't blame him . . . I mean, after what happened to us tonight."

My jaw tightened at the thought. "Funny how your mind can play tricks on you," I said. "I never heard a bear make sounds like that before in my life. But then, I never stood between a hungry bear and its dinner before, either. I have to admit, my imagination got the best of me. How about you, Joe? Did you think it was a big cat? You never said."

"It had me fooled too, Bill."

I looked at him. His face sincere. Still, I couldn't help but wonder if he was just trying to make me feel better.

"Oh and by the way," he added. "You're not going to write about this in one of your books, are you?"

I glanced at him, then fixed my eyes on the highway ahead, fingers methodically drumming the steering wheel.

"Bill . . . ?"

I could feel his eyes on me as I sat in stony silence, purposely cocking my head back and forth, debating an answer.

After a long moment: "You are, aren't you!"

31

"Nah," I said with a shrug of finality. "Why embarrass myself. Besides, it probably wouldn't make a good story anyway . . . would it?"

Author's Notes

On March 2, 2011, the U.S. Fish and Wildlife Service announced that the eastern cougar (puma concolor couguar), a subspecies of the larger cougar family which has been on the endangered species list since 1973, is extinct. The Service conducted a formal review of scientific literature from the U.S. and Canada, and requested information from the twenty-one states within the historical range of the subspecies. None of the states believed in the existence of an eastern cougar population. As a result, the Service concluded that the eastern cougar is extinct and should be removed from the endangered species list. The Florida panther (puma concolor coryi), a different but related subspecies, remains an endangered species with only eighty to one hundred adult panthers left in the wild.

On June 11, 2011, the first confirmed wild mountain lion in Connecticut in more than one hundred years was killed when it was struck by a sport utility vehicle on the Wilbur Cross Parkway near Milford. DNA from its hair and scat samples showed that it had passed through Minnesota and Wisconsin in 2009 and 2010 as it traveled halfway across the country from South Dakota. The two-thousand mile journey was one of the longest ever recorded for a land mammal. Genetic tests confirmed that the cat, a one hundred and forty pound male, had the same genetic structure as the mountain lion population in South Dakota's Black Hills region.

Didst thou never hear
That things ill got had ever bad success?

~Shakespeare

Unintended Consequences

EVER HAVE SOMETHING HAPPEN that you can't seem to forget? Some relatively small but unpleasant thing that lingers in the folds of your brain? For years on end?

I have.

And though it happened long ago, in my early time as a game warden, the memory of it keeps coming back to me like a recurring bad dream.

I'd been patrolling Wyoming County with Deputy Gene Gaydos since before dawn, and had just pulled into a local restaurant for dinner, when headquarters contacted me by radio: two deer shot by poachers at a nearby farm; we were to proceed immediately. My stomach growled in angry protest as I made a reluctant U-turn and started back out on the highway.

It was the first Saturday of buck season. With over one million licenses sold to Pennsylvania deer hunters, game wardens are run ragged. Radio communications become a blur of complaints on illegal hunting activity—some real, some imagined—with every complainant demanding we respond immediately. Difficult at best, considering most wardens have approximately four hundred square miles of real estate to cover. Hopefully there are no hunting accidents.

Even a minor one can take hours to investigate; a fatal might tie you up for days, leaving your district wide open for poachers to commit their mayhem.

Darkness was setting in fast when we arrived at the farm. I steered into a dirt lane and followed it back toward an old and weathered brown barn. Two men stood outside. One had a scoped Winchester rifle cradled in his arms. Upon seeing my patrol vehicle, he leaned it against the barn wall and waved us over. A large man with a fierce black beard and thick bushy eyebrows, he wore a checkered shirt and camo hunting pants cinched up by wide suspenders that were stretched to the breaking point over his broad belly.

After parking next to the barn, my deputy and I started toward the men when a pickup truck pulled into the property and beeped its horn as it came toward us. There was a lone driver inside. He pulled alongside us and rolled down a window.

"Thanks for coming so fast. Had to drive all the way to the Hilltop Store to make the call. No phone here."

I nodded appreciatively. "Your name, sir?"

"Denver Jones. I own the place." He was gaunt and tanned. A face mapped with wrinkles from years in the sun. He climbed from the truck and poked out a hand. We shook briefly. "Used to be a thriving farm once," he said. "Now all that's left is an old barn and a hundred acres of open field."

"A lot of that going around these days. It's too bad."

Jones nodded briskly, then moved his eyes to the dim horizon. He bore the lost look of a castaway searching an endless sea. "Don't pay to farm no more," he said, shaking his head with sorrow.

Denver Jones was not alone in his assessment. Wyoming County had more than its share of farms long since abandoned. Many dairy farmers, plagued for years with low milk prices, had sold their cows and quit altogether. But the reverting crop fields that dotted the county grew thick with tender saplings and tall grasses, affording food and cover for many game species, especially the Commonwealth's burgeoning deer herd.

"I understand you had a run-in with some poachers," I said. "Two deer shot?"

He jerked his head at the two men by the barn. "They hung 'em inside for safe keeping. They'll tell you all about it."

As we turned toward them, a young German shorthaired pointer suddenly burst from behind the barn. A handsome dog, colored liver and white. And when he saw Gaydos and me, he made a high-spirited charge directly for us.

"Don't worry," the big man called out, "he won't hurt you; he's just a pup."

I knew all about hunting dogs; this breed was one of the most energetic—a dog that loved people, too. Consequently, the only thing that worried me was how my uniform would fare after the happy-go-lucky pup finished dancing all over me.

But the big man proved his great size made him no less agile as he quickly intercepted the pointer. Holding him by the collar, he knelt down and whispered a few words to the adolescent dog. The pup sat immediately. He was nose to nose with his master now, ears tilted forward in eager anticipation, muscular thighs quivering with excitement. The bearded man dug into his pocket, fished out a biscuit, and held it directly in front of the pup. "Now, watch this," he said, glancing at me. After feeding him the treat, he uttered a soft command. The pointer, seeming to understand, cocked his head as if in protest.

"You heard me," the bearded man insisted. The pup gave Gaydos and me a quick look and then turned to scamper off behind the barn once more.

"Impressive!" I said.

"Name's Fritz." He stood and stuck out his hand.

We shook, my meager fist vanishing in his clasp. "I'm Wasserman, Mr. Fritz. This is my partner, Deputy Gaydos."

The leviathan looked at me and frowned. "Fritz is my dog. My name is Baker. Jimmy Baker." He cocked his head toward the other. "This is my friend, Derek."

Of medium height and narrow in frame, Derek gazed at me with yawning blue eyes that had an almost eerie intensity. A man effeminate in appearance, his ample hair, blonde and well groomed, spilled to his shoulders in a cascade of tight curls. A bright gold earring dangled from one ear.

I nodded a greeting and turned to Baker. "What do you know about the deer that were killed here?"

"I can tell you one thing right off the bat: we're from Jersey and *we* have more respect for wildlife than the local yokels who live here, know what I'm sayin'?" He glanced at Derek, who prompted him on with an urgent nod. "Anyway, Derek and me, we were just getting started when three shots came from back in the woods. Nobody's supposed to hunt here but us, so we went out to see who it was. We spotted two hunters. I hollered at 'em that they were on private property and they took off." Baker looked at Denver Jones, who had walked up behind me to listen in, then shrugged his heavy shoulders in a gesture of blamelessness. "They took off in a hurry, too."

"Get a look at them?" I asked.

"Nope. They were too far away. No sense chasing after them, either. I'm too out of shape to run."

"How about their clothes? Do you remember what they were wearing?"

"They were dressed in camouflage, top to bottom. Locals, too. No truck, no car, no four-wheeler—nothing." He cursed under his breath. "Came on foot. Sneaky devils. We hiked down to where we saw them and found two dead doe." Baker paused, his look turning sour. "Derek unzipped them so they wouldn't go to waste. I gotta admit I never had the stomach for that part of it."

I glanced at frail Derek, his face exuding a self-important smile.

"I helped haul 'em and hang 'em, though," said Baker. "Then we called you guys out here because we didn't want to be accused of anything, know what I'm sayin'? The locals want to blame us Jersey guys for killing all the deer, but they're the ones shooting everything, not us. Derek and I never even got a chance to hunt today."

Baker came across like he was on the level. After all, a late model Buick with New Jersey tags was parked next to the barn. He and Derek could have stuffed both deer into the trunk and been heading for the state line long ago.

"Sorry your hunting plans were ruined," I said. "But we do appreciate that you and Derek gave up your time in order to get involved with this case."

"No big deal. Just wanted to do what's right, know what I'm sayin'?"

"I understand you put the deer in the barn."

"Safe and sound!" he declared.

"Let's take a look."

The big man spun on his heels. He gestured for us to follow him and his willowy companion into the barn. As we stepped inside, there was the familiar scent of leather and earth along with the musky tang of eviscerated big game. Here two gutted deer hung by their necks from a heavy wooden beam by the door. Both were yearling doe, most likely siblings. I removed a cigar-sized flashlight from a pouch on my belt and directed its beam over both carcasses. Each deer had been shot in the chest by a single projectile. The entrance wounds looked to be from a thirty caliber rifle, one of the most popular cartridge groups in the world. In addition, both bullets had passed clean through their intended targets to sail into oblivion, leaving no chance for a slug to match to a suspect's gun.

Darkness had set in. The moonless night would make it extremely difficult to pick up leads back in the woods where the deer had been killed. For the time being, there was little I could do but obtain identification from the men and continue my investigation the following day.

"Will you be here tomorrow?" I asked Baker.

"Nope. We're heading back to New Jersey soon as you leave. But we'll be here next weekend. We got tags to fill, know what I'm sayin?"

I nodded. "Fair enough. But if you think of anything that could help us find who did this, I want you to give me a call."

"You can count on it! We want these guys even more than you do."

I doubted it.

After jotting down hunting licenses and the necessary contact information from our two informants, Gaydos and I lowered both deer to the ground and dragged the carcasses over to my patrol car.

Suddenly, Baker's dog bolted from the shadows and came galloping straight at us. Graceful and well balanced, with a deep chest and powerful quarters, he bore the look of a champion in the making. He stopped dead in his tracks when he got within a few feet.

"Hey, Fritz!" I called.

He wagged his stubbed tail and whined excitedly while keeping his feet planted as if frozen to the ground.

"I think Fritz is a little leery of the deer," I said.

Gaydos smiled. "He's waiting for them to jump up and come back to life."

We loaded both deer on the steel big game rack attached to my rear bumper and began securing the carcasses with rubber bungee cords while Fritz barked with grand bravado, pacing just out of reach. When we finished lashing down the deer, I swiveled toward the young pointer and dropped to one knee. "Come here, boy," I said cheerily. "I'm not gonna hurt you." Reaching into my coat pocket, I retrieved a dog biscuit and offered it at arm's length. "C'mon boy!"

Fritz stood his ground and cocked his head curiously, dewy eyes glued to the bait in my hand.

"Emergency rations?" asked Gaydos.

"Kind of . . . they saved my butt a few times with aggressive dogs." I leaned forward and clicked my tongue. "Here, Fritz!"

Still leery of the deer, he backed away on stiff legs. He circled my vehicle, muzzle in the air, nostrils quivering as he inhaled their pungent scent. He made two loops before stopping again. This time slightly more than a yard separated us.

"Good boy," I cooed. "Come and get it."

Fritz woofed at me and sat stubbornly, a low, piteous whine rising in the back of his throat. I tossed the biscuit between his front paws. He dropped his head and took it with his tongue, champing the treat greedily with his rear molars before swallowing. I dug into my pocket for another and held it out, certain he couldn't resist after eating the first. "You'll have to come and get this one."

Fritz cocked his head at me as if I'd just sprouted horns.

"Don't look at me like that." And in a gesture of theatrical finality, I stretched my coat pocket wide and dangled the biscuit above for a tantalizing moment before dropping it inside.

Fritz sprang to his feet and pattered to me. He wagged his hind-end and nudged my pocket with a damp muzzle.

"Okay, okay," I chuckled, digging out another biscuit. "I was just kidding—"

"Spoiling my dog, are ya?"

I swiveled to see Jimmy Baker approaching, a huge smile pushing through his thick beard.

"Couldn't help myself; he's pretty hard to resist."

Baker's face lit up. "I know, I know. Everybody loves Fritz! But I can't let you take him home with you."

"Afraid you would say that," I said. I massaged Fritz's ears with my fingers and looked into his handsome face. "Hear that, ol' buddy? You have to stay here."

Fritz wagged his tail and lapped my chin with a warm, wet tongue. His breath smelled of Milk-Bones.

"Okay, Mr. Baker," I said, rising to my feet. "We're heading out. But we'll be in touch."

"You got my number, warden. I'll be on dayshift next week; if you call, make sure it's after six o'clock, know what I'm sayin'?"

Gaydos and I had just left the farm and were driving along the state road when a truck with a pleasure boat in tow came hurtling toward us in the opposite lane. I felt my vehicle sway as the rig whooshed by.

I glanced into my side mirror and watched its tail lights disappear into the night. "Someone's in a hurry."

"Accident waiting to happen," grunted my deputy.

"Odd, too."

"What?"

"The boat."

Gaydos considered this for a moment. "Now that you mention it, you don't see many Cobalt Bowriders around here, especially twenty-five-footers."

I was surprised he'd been able to identify the vessel, especially at night. It had blasted by in seconds. But I wasn't commenting on the make or model. I hardly knew one from another. I just thought it odd to see *any* boat in late December when the lakes were covered with ice. I kept it to myself.

"Hungry?" I asked.

"Little bit."

"Me too."

Weary from the long day, we continued toward town in mutual silence until we came to the restaurant I had detoured earlier. I pulled in and parked. Inside, the place was bustling with hunters, every table taken. Gaydos spotted two empty stools at the far counter. We headed straight for them amid the clatter of dishes and the lively chatter about deer hunting. Hunters dressed in camos and blaze orange gawked openly as we passed by. We were used to it, especially during deer season when legions of hunters—many from out of state—infiltrated the county. Most had probably never seen a uniformed game warden before. One bewhiskered man stopped mid-bite into a sandwich, his eyes flitting nervously between Gaydos and me before looking out a side window. Somewhere in the well-lit parking lot would be his vehicle. I wondered what contraband it might hold.

We sat at the counter, our backs to the curious onlookers while studying our menus. The place was famous for its burgers and homemade deserts, so we each ordered the Hamburger Special with a Side O' Fries. I asked for coffee ahead of my meal. Gaydos ordered tea, as usual.

I closed my menu and had just handed it to our waitress when a voice came from behind us: "You're just the guys I've been looking for!" Gaydos and I turned simultaneously to see a rawboned man in his forties with a young boy whom I assumed was his son. Both were dressed in camo-orange fatigues.

"Can I help you?"

"Hope so. I want to report a violation: hunting over bait." His bronze, weather-hardened face was lined with concern. A group of four hunters stared at us from a nearby table where two chairs stood empty. The only vacant seats in the restaurant, they obviously belonged to our visitors.

Tips on poaching are not uncommon during hunting season. But experience told me they often don't pan out. Many prove to be unsubstantiated rumors or information too vague to act on. I remained skeptical.

"Where is this baiting taking place?" I asked.

The man glanced down at the boy and frowned. "Best go back to your chair, son. This is grownups' business."

His face fell as he turned and marched back to the table where the four hunters sat. One man reached out and ruffled his hair apologetically as they watched us from their chairs.

So as not to be overheard, the informant leaned in, lowering his voice. "Do you know where the Empty Pot Camp is, up on Blacksnake Mountain?"

Gaydos and I exchanged glances. We'd been getting tips of poaching activity at the camp for years but were never able to confirm anything. "We're familiar with it," I said.

"Good!" His eyes glittered with approval. "Would've lost faith in you otherwise. Then you must also know about the brood of vipers that hunt out of that place. Bunch of lazy game hogs."

"We're aware of them, sir."

He nodded appreciatively. "Suspected as much. Last year I came across the tracks of a huge buck up there. Followed them through the snow for over a mile. Be danged if they didn't take me right to the camp. Big pile of apples out back. Looked like maybe half a ton. Deer droppings and trails everywhere too—"

"Excuse me," I broke in. "Did you say *last* year?"

He paused and blinked at me. " . . . Yeah . . . first day of buck season."

"Why didn't you contact us *then?*"

"Because you're the first game wardens I've seen since then."

Didn't this guy ever hear of a telephone?

"Have you been up there at all this year?" I asked, hoping he might still have some timely information.

"Nah. Decided to hunt someplace else. I don't want to be on the same mountain with that bunch."

I sighed within. "Appreciate the information, sir. We'll check it out. But deer season's been open for a week. Good chance they've been to the camp and gone already." I opened my wallet and pulled out a business card. "Next time you see a violation, call me right away, okay?"

He pinched the card with two bony fingers and stuffed it into his pocket. "Now that I know how to reach you . . . sure, you can count on it."

There was the gentle rattle of dishware being set on the counter behind me. "Anything else?" I asked.

"No, no, no. I don't want to interrupt your meal. Appreciate your time, officer." He turned and walked back to his table. I watched as he sat down with his friends, their voices low and heavy with excitement. The boy looked up and gazed at me brightly. So proud of his father. I smiled and offered him an assuring nod, then swiveled on my chair and reached for my coffee.

Gaydos squeezed his tea bag into a spoon and watched the auburn liquid drip into his cup. "Can't help but wonder about guys like that."

"Makes two of us. I'd love to catch the Empty Pot Gang hunting over bait."

"We've been at this a long time, and it's the same thing every year. I'll never understand why some people see a violation and then wait till the next hunting season to report it."

"They're scared, Gene. They hate what they see, but they're afraid to get involved. Then they spot a game warden someplace and their conscience starts bothering them. So they walk over and tell him about it, get the matter off their chest."

Gaydos raised his cup to his lips and paused in reflection. "So you're saying we absolve them of their sins, so to speak, huh?"

"Never really thought of it like that—but yes, now that you mention it."

He took a mouthful of tea and swallowed. Looking over his cup, he said, "How about I head over to the Empty Pot Camp tomorrow and see if they're still around. Might find fresh bait that could lead to some arrests."

"Sounds like a plan."

We both knew it would be better if he checked the camp without me. I was too well known in the county, too easily recognized, even when out of uniform. Instead, Gaydos would dress in hunting clothes and take his personal vehicle, as he often would over the years, in order to get a close look at a suspected poacher's property.

The crowd meant dinner would be slow in coming, so we sipped our cups and talked about Baker and Derek. Gaydos said he'd head back to Denver Jones's farm at first light tomorrow, before checking the Empty Pot Camp. He wanted to visit the crime scene while any remaining evidence would still be fresh. If the poachers were local, as Baker had suggested, he might be able to track them back to their homes, might even run into a witness who'd seen something suspicious. Although it would be a Sunday, I had plenty of loose ends to deal with regarding prior investigations, and was grateful that my deputy had volunteered to do all the legwork. But I wasn't surprised. Deputy Gaydos had proven his dedication to the Pennsylvania Game Commission and our natural resources time and again over the many years I'd known him.

Gene Gaydos called the next morning to report bad news: "I checked out the Empty Pot Camp," he said. "The place was empty. We missed them, Bill. There must have been a hundred apples scattered out back. I found blood trails leading away from the bait. Looks like they got two deer." He muttered something under his breath. "I didn't spend much time snooping around. Didn't want to risk someone spotting me from a neighboring camp and then tipping them off. They might be back later in the week."

I felt my blood pressure kick up a notch. Had our informant warned us earlier, we might have been able to catch them in the act. Disappointed, I asked Gaydos to keep an eye on the camp for the remainder of the season.

"You can count on it. It's just a matter of time before we get them."

But my deputy had even more bad news as he related his investigation into the Jones property: He said he'd been all over the area where the deer were killed and had found two fresh gut piles in the woods a hundred yards from the barn. He backtracked them to the kill sites. Both deer had been shot in an open field before running into the trees to die. Gaydos thought it highly unlikely someone living in the area had been responsible. If they were on foot, as Baker had claimed, they would have come in from the back of the farm, avoiding the barn and main highway. The terrain was rugged and steep here. It would've taken a monumental effort to drag the heavy carcasses to the nearest back road. And Gaydos assured me that the "local yokels," as Baker had so eloquently referred to them, weren't so dumb.

" . . . On my way back, I picked up some .308 shell casings," he said. "They were lying by a foot path leading to the barn. Fresh and shiny, too."

"Baker had a .308 rifle!" I said. "Can't be a coincidence."

"Thought the same thing when I found the shells. I think Baker started down the path, spotted two deer standing in the open, and couldn't resist. Looks like he fired three times, missed once. Not bad considering the distance."

"But if Baker killed them, why call us? Why not just hightail it back to New Jersey?"

"Thought about that, too. I figure that's what they intended, but they were sidetracked by Denver Jones. Bumped into him while I was out there. Had a little chat. Turns out he'd been running errands yesterday and stopped by the farm unexpectedly only to find Baker and Derek dragging two deer out of the field."

The news hit me like a blow to the head. I'd assumed that Jones had been with Baker and Derek all along, but it was by mere chance that he'd blundered into them before they could make off with the deer. Caught red-handed, they'd come up with a story about trespassers killing the deer to cover themselves.

"I can't believe Jones didn't tell us about this last night," I groaned. "It changes everything."

"Would've made all the difference in the world," agreed Gaydos. "But it seems that Mr. Jones is a trusting soul. The idea that Baker and his pal might have killed the deer themselves, never entered his head."

But it should have entered my *head,* I thought. Instead, I had allowed two poachers to escape into New Jersey. Like most states, Pennsylvania doesn't extradite suspects for wildlife crimes. They were home free. I immediately began to doubt my ability as an investigator. Most lawmen were cynics—or at the very least, skeptics at heart. That's what makes them good cops; it's what makes them dig in, get to the bottom of things, come up with results.

"Should've questioned Jones further last night," I muttered into the phone. "Pressed him for more details."

"Whoa, Bill—they fooled me too. Don't lay everything on *your* shoulders. We're putting too many hours in, not getting enough downtime. It's starting to take a toll."

Gaydos was right. We'd been working day and night for weeks on end; both of us suffered from burnout. "Another week and it'll start winding down," I said, ignoring the temptation to take the rest of the day off, give my bones a rest. "Does Jones know we suspect his two hunting guests?"

"Nope. I kept a straight face when he told me how things went down."

"Excellent."

"So now what?"

I tapped the plastic handset against my chin in soft, measured beats while considering my options. "Buck season ends next Saturday," I said. "It'll be their last chance to take a deer. I'm going to call Baker. Play dumb. Try to convince him it's still okay to come back."

"Won't be easy. They gotta suspect we're on to them by now."

"Either that or we're just a couple of dopey local yokels."

Gaydos chuckled into the phone: "Barney Fife and Gomer Pyle, right?"

"Exactly. And I intend to convince Baker of just that."

"Good luck," said Gaydos. "I hope you can pull it off."

I hung up and stared back at the phone as if it held the key to the words I needed to get Baker to return. Although he had assured me last night at the farm that he'd be back next weekend, I doubted he really meant it. Baker had snookered me into believing that he and Derek were innocent bystanders, trustworthy informants; and now he was home scot-free. For all I knew, he was already crowing to his friends about pulling one over on the warden. And, I figured, in that case I had nothing to lose by contacting him. My phone call would make no difference whatsoever—other than to give him another opportunity to gloat over the fact that he'd tricked me. But what if he was sitting at home right now, all warm and comfy with the notion that Gaydos and I actually believed him—that he was indeed a trustworthy informant. What if he wanted to come back for a crack at another deer, but a tiny voice inside his head kept telling him to stay in New Jersey, not to risk it, to assume nothing. What if he just needed a gentle prod, a tiny reassurance that it was okay to return—or better yet, a *reason* to return.

And that was precisely what I intended to give him as I picked up the receiver and dialed long distance to Camden.

Baker sounded different. His voice weak and ragged when he spoke. If I didn't know better, I would have thought he was a much smaller man. There was a touch of melancholy too, in his words. I assumed, because he'd been caught off guard, my call had him flustered, for he'd lost the jubilant, booming personality he'd possessed only yesterday.

"Officer Wasserman!" he breathed. "Didn't expect to hear from you so soon."

"I wanted to give you an update on our investigation. It's not going well. We need your help."

Baker hesitated. "Help . . . ? In what way?"

"Every investigation starts with a crime scene," I informed him. "That means we have to begin looking at things from where the deer were killed on the property and go on from there. Unfortunately, we can't find the gut piles. Coyotes and vultures must have gotten to them."

Baker said nothing.

"I have a metal detector. It's a good one. I'd like to search for spent shell casings—maybe even a bullet, since both deer were shot clean through. But I don't know where to start; it could take *weeks* to find anything. I'm going to need you to show me exactly where the deer were killed when you come back next Saturday. Was hoping you wouldn't mind sacrificing a little more of your time."

Seconds ticked like minutes before Baker finally replied: "Look . . . this call . . . it's bad timing. I've just suffered the loss of a friend. I can't think straight right now."

"Sorry to hear that. Hope you don't mind me asking . . . Derek?"

"No. Not him. Look . . . I'll see you next Saturday, okay?"

"Appreciate it. Thanks. What time?"

"Later in the afternoon."

"Two o'clock?"

"Yeah. Sure. See you then."

There was a click, followed by the drone of a line gone dead. The melancholy hum matched my feelings perfectly, because a tiny voice inside my head whispered that Baker knew I was on to him, and that he would never set foot into Pennsylvania again.

Adrift in a sea of legal research for an upcoming bear poaching trial, I reached across my cluttered desk and answered the phone with a distracted grumble.

"Bill . . . ? Is that you?"

I recognized the voice: a Game Commission dispatcher. "Hey, Barney. It's me all right."

"Sorry, didn't sound like you."

"It's called sleep deprivation," I said with a dry chuckle.

"Tell me about it. Most officers are putting in eighteen-hour days. Bet you'll be glad to see the season come to an end."

"Yep. Counting down. What do you have for me?" I asked.

"Guy who calls himself Derek wants to talk to you. And get this: when I asked for his last name, he said he didn't have one! Said you'd know who he was."

"I know him all right."

"What does this guy think, he's famous, another Cher or Oprah?"

"I guess. Actually, I checked his driver's license last Saturday; believe it or not, the man only *has* one name."

"Rock star, huh?"

"Who knows? Kinda looks like one. Got a phone number?"

"It's long distance. New Jersey."

I jotted down the number and hung up. It had been two days since I'd spoken with Jimmy Baker, for what I presumed would be the last time I'd ever speak to him again, and I found it nothing less than remarkable that his friend, Derek, wanted to chat with me now. At the Jones property, Baker had done all the talking while his diminutive companion regarded him with a quiet reverence, his intense gaze drinking Baker's every spoken word. I wondered what he'd have to say. Perhaps he'd been mulling things over since Saturday and wanted to get the matter off his chest, clear his conscience. It was possible, I thought, that he'd been dragged into the entire affair by Baker, that he'd been reluctant to speak up around his huge companion, afraid to tell us what really happened that day. So it was with great expectations that I lifted the handset back off its cradle and dialed.

The phone rang twice. "Warehouse," answered a nasally male voice.

I said that I represented the Pennsylvania Game Commission and wanted to speak with Derek.

"You're Wasserman, right?" the voice said expectantly.

"Yes, who are you?"

"Name's Sam. I'm in the cleaning business with Derek. He told me you'd be calling." His thin, whiney tone sounded vaguely familiar, but I quickly shrugged it off as nothing more than a hard New Jersey accent. "You just missed him," he said. "Stepped out a minute ago."

I wasn't happy with the news. When a suspect decides he wants to talk, it often means an admission of guilt, or at the very least, that significant new information about the case will be forthcoming. But it's crucial for the officer to respond quickly or risk having the individual change his mind after consulting with some local barroom "lawyer" willing to dole out free advice to anyone who buys him a drink.

"Derek told me all about the incident," the voice went on "—how he and Jimmy chased two armed poachers off the property, how they took the time to gut the deer they'd killed and transport them to a safe place until the wardens arrived. You were there that day, weren't you?"

"Yes."

"That was pretty decent of them, I mean, giving up their hunting time and all. They should be commended, don't you think?"

"Absolutely!" I declared. "And I plan on doing just that when I see them on Saturday."

"Did you catch the guys who did it yet?"

"We're working on it."

"Any idea who they might be?"

"Not a clue."

"Well, Derek thinks you suspect him and Jimmy. He's worried sick about it, too. Said they never should've got involved."

I ignored the remark. "When will Derek be back?"

"I don't know!" he said, his thin voice turning more shrill. "But I'll tell you what I *do* know: they could have left those deer to rot in the woods, but they wanted to do the right thing, know what I'm sayin'?—Preserve the meat so it wouldn't go to waste."

My stomach dropped into my lap.

Baker!

He'd been disguising his voice, pretending to be someone else. Like some goofy high school sophomore hiding from the truant officer. His bizarre conduct took me by surprise, and I began to question his mental stability.

"Time to stop the charade, Mr. Baker. I know it's you."

There was a long silence, followed by two garbled voices in the background, the conversation frantic. Baker and Derek arguing, I reasoned. And I waited for the line to go dead.

Instead, Baker returned, and after an impatient sigh, he cleared his throat and began talking to me in his natural

50

voice: "Look, Wasserman, you got nothing on Derek and me, so why don't you stop harassing us? We didn't do anything wrong. We were just trying to help, and now this is the thanks we get!" He paused for a moment, his breathing labored. "The locals are always trespassing on Denver's property. We post it every year; and every year they tear down the signs, shoot up the barn, and hunt on us. Why don't you do your job and go after *them*? They're the ones responsible for killing all your precious deer."

"The locals didn't kill anything, Mr. Baker. You did. That became clear to me after we found .308 shell casings at the crime scene."

"Not from *my* gun, you didn't!"

"Well, then why don't you come back to Pennsylvania and hand over your Winchester so we can run a ballistics check? If you're telling the truth, it would clear you of any wrongdoing."

A long silence passed, broken finally—astonishingly—by a storm of heartrending sobs.

I listened in a stunned hush. What had happened to this man? His behavior so irrational, so odd. Now this sudden breakdown. He seemed an emotional wreck.

And suddenly, I knew: "Fritz is dead!" he howled. "Isn't he payment enough for your two lousy deer?"

I felt my chest close like a vise. The few minutes I'd spent with the young pointer had spawned a strong fondness for him. I was sickened by the news.

"He was a good dog," I offered "Sorry to hear that."

I paused and considered Baker's tone. It almost sounded like he was blaming me for the death of his dog. "What do you mean by 'payment enough?'" I asked.

Baker expelled a long, shuddering breath. "I only looked away for a second. I swear. That's all it was. Then I saw him chasing after your car. He was already halfway down the driveway. I called out, and he stopped to look back . . . then he was gone!" Baker's voice fell into a ragged whisper. "He got hit, man. Hit hard. I'll never get the sound out of my head: that sickening smack—Fritz's yelp." He chuckled

51

bitterly. "Didn't even get to finish it. The yelp, I mean. It was cut off. So I knew. Knew before I got to the road, that he was gone. I got there just in time to see the truck. It was hauling a boat. Flying! Never even slowed down. Fritz was lying dead in the middle of the road and the guy never even slows down. What do you make of somebody like that?"

I remembered the heavy-bodied pickup that came speeding toward Gaydos and me after I pulled onto the state highway, the oncoming glow of its headlights in the night, its wake rocking my car as it blasted by with a huge boat in tow.

And I tried to ignore the creeping guilt that wormed through my brain.

Fritz is dead . . . I saw him chasing after your car.

"Did you get a license number?"

"Never even thought about it. After seeing Fritz like that I just froze. Guess it was shock or something."

"I understand."

I couldn't help but wonder if Fritz would still be alive had I not won his trust by feeding him biscuits. And what about the deer on my rack . . . every dog loves to chase deer. Why didn't I check to see if Fritz was following me before I drove onto the highway?

We're putting too many hours in . . . It's starting to take a toll.

I quickly shook the guilt from my head. Baker was simply looking for a scapegoat. Although I regretted not being more careful with his dog, it was Baker's responsibility to control Fritz, not mine. In truth, he had no one to blame but himself. Had Baker not killed two illegal deer, I wouldn't have been summoned to the property in the first place. But in typical outlaw fashion, Baker looked to blame someone else for his mistakes.

"Look, Mr. Baker," I said. "I'm really sorry to hear about Fritz, but I want you to know that I intend to file criminal charges against you and Derek for the unlawful killing of two antlerless deer."

Baker exploded into the phone: "What! Are you crazy? You got no proof, no witnesses, nothing! Nobody saw us kill any deer. No way you can pin this on us!"

"It's called circumstantial evidence, Mr. Baker. Just because nobody saw you doesn't mean you won't be—"

"Hey! This is still America, pal. I don't care what kind of kangaroo court you got up there in the sticks, you still gotta prove I'm guilty, know what I'm sayin'?"

"I know what you're saying all right. Now listen to what I'm saying: The only thing I have to prove is that you and Derek were in *possession* of two unlawfully killed deer. It's not necessary to prove you killed them—although we both know you did."

"I ain't guilty of nothing! Neither is Derek."

"You're going to have to convince a judge of that," I said. "Just make sure you have a good attorney. You'll need one."

"I'll see you in court, pal. I'm calling my lawyer right now; and when this is over I'm gonna sue you for harassment."

Later that week, I filed citations against Jimmy Baker and his friend, Derek, for possession of two unlawfully killed deer. Each man faced a heavy fine and revocation of his hunting privileges. A trial date was set for the two accused poachers and, as promised, Baker hired a lawyer.

But on the day they were to appear in court, neither Jimmy Baker nor Derek bothered to show. The defense attorney claimed that it would be a hardship for his clients to travel from New Jersey for a hearing and asked the judge to hold the trial *in absentia* (legal jargon meaning in absence of the defendants). The judge gave her consent, and the trial proceeded.

This wasn't the first time that I had prosecuted a case in the absence of a defendant. It usually made my job easy. Hearings in absentia typically involved minor game law infractions with small penalties, like late spotlighting or hunting with an unplugged shotgun. And, because no one shows up in court to defend themselves, all I have to do is testify to what I saw: "*Your Honor, I observed the defendant unlawfully spotlighting deer at two in the morning . . .*"

Voilá. Guilty!

But this was a serious poaching incident with relatively high fines and the potential loss of hunting licenses. It involved not one, but two suspects. And, unlike my other trials in absentia, this one involved a defense attorney. (I later asked him if he'd ever defended someone who didn't appear for his own trial before. He told me he hadn't.) All things considered, I was stunned to find that neither defendant would appear in court.

Still, this would be no simple case. Even the most inept attorney can complicate a trial by asking artful questions designed to confuse witnesses. Testimony from a credible eyewitness can be extremely persuasive to a judge or jury; hence, the defense attorney tries his best to befuddle anyone who takes the stand against his client.

But when Denver Jones testified that he'd inadvertently bumped into Baker and Derek dragging two illegal deer into his barn, and that he'd believed their story about trespassers being responsible for the poaching incident, the defense attorney had no reason to challenge him. Jones had made no accusations against his clients. He simply declared what he saw that day and stated that he believed they were telling him the truth when they said someone else had killed the deer.

Nevertheless, I considered it important testimony, for it demonstrated that Jones had caught Baker and Derek by surprise, lending credence to my allegation that they'd come up with the tale about trespassers in order to justify their possession of the two illegal deer.

After Denver Jones stepped from the witness chair, Deputy Gaydos and I each had an opportunity to testify. The defense attorney cross-examined us, attempting to poke holes in our statements; and although he tried diligently to get his clients off the hook, when the judge took everything into consideration: the shell casings found at the scene, entry wounds in both deer that likely came from a .308 bullet, Baker's shenanigans on the phone, and the fact that he and Derek had been caught red-handed with the illegal deer (that Baker and Derek refused to appear in court could not have helped their case), she found both men guilty as charged and sentenced them each to pay a thousand dollar fine and receive three years revocation of their hunting privileges.

Neither Baker nor Derek ever paid the court-ordered fines (although I suspect they paid their attorney fees, which had to be substantial). As a result, their hunting licenses were revoked indefinitely and warrants were issued for their arrests. Unfortunately, I never saw the men again, and the warrants remain open to this day.

Still, I am haunted by the memory of a playful and intelligent young gundog named Fritz, with his dewy brown eyes and delightful spirit. A striking animal to behold. So vibrant. So full of life.

Too, I remember Baker's ragged cry:

Fritz is dead! Isn't he payment enough?

And in the end, I must confess, sadly, I believe he was.

A Valentine's Surprise

SHE **HAD BEEN WATCHING** the truck from her kitchen window since it pulled into the driveway and stopped there. At first, she thought it would back up and turn around. Someone lost, perhaps. Instead, the passenger door opened and a man jumped out. He stepped quickly to the back. Just behind the cab was a large metal box spanning the bed. He opened the lid and began to reach inside.

Emma Boggs spun around to call her husband. "Marcus! Come quick!"

He'd been sitting in the den, reading all afternoon.

Fool's more interested in Wall Street than in his own back yard!

She turned to peer out the window once more. So fast! The man already back inside the truck. His hand on the door as he closed it behind him.

"Marcus!"

Marcus Boggs folded his newspaper and dropped it on the mahogany coffee table. He pushed himself off his favorite chair, a plush, leather recliner purchased decades ago, and shuffled toward the kitchen. They weren't expecting company. Who could it be?

Emma Boggs stood by the window, her gaping eyes locked on the pickup truck. It began moving toward her house now. Two men inside.

What in the world was wrong with them? Couldn't they see the "No Trespassing" signs?

"Marcus, hurry!" she cried.

But Marcus Boggs was long past the days when he could hurry to go anywhere. His twisted back bothered him more than ever lately. Although he'd been seeing a chiropractor for the last six months, the visits didn't seem to be helping much. He found it especially troublesome to get around after he'd been lazing in his recliner. And as he scuffed toward the kitchen to see what his wife was squawking about, a familiar painful tingling began to radiate from his buttocks down to the ball of his left foot.

As Emma Boggs watched the black pickup ease to a stop, her aging heart fluttered with dread. Directly across from the truck, three wild turkeys pecked on cracked corn that had been left by her husband, fleshy blue heads bobbing erratically. So intent was their feeding, they never noticed as the driver opened his door and slipped from the vehicle. A rifle in his hands.

Oh no! No, no, no! This could not be happening! Not here! Not now! Her mouth fell open in horror. She wrung her hands beneath her chin. Squeezing so tightly they ached.

"MAAAAARCUUUUS!"

W hen Jed spotted the turkeys from the state highway, Bo made a quick left into a dirt lane and stopped. "Gun's in the tool chest," he said. "Go ahead and get it."

Jed shouldered open the door and hustled to the back of the truck. He reached over and popped open the lid on the big aluminum tool bin and grabbed a twenty-two caliber rifle. Then he quickly got back inside with Bo. "They're just around the bend up ahead. Three gobblers. Nice big ones too. Another fifty yards and you'll seem them."

Bo scanned the property, an anxious look in his eyes. The fields on each side of them were freshly mowed. The lane they were on was narrower than most roads. "You sure this ain't somebody's driveway?"

Jed shrugged. "Sign said 'Boggs Road' back where we turned in. Now, let's go before the birds take off."

Bo took his foot off the brake and bumped the gas. As Jed had promised, there were three fine gobblers as soon as he rounded the bend. He grabbed his binoculars off the dashboard and adjusted the eyepiece. In the bright sunlight, their bronze feathers gleamed with blue and green highlights.

"Look at the size of them!" yelped Bo. "They gotta be twenty pounders, at least."

"Whatever they're eating sure must be good," said Jed. "They ain't paying us no mind at all. Bet you could nail one from right here."

Bo bunched his lips and slowly lowered the binoculars. A house stood directly behind the gobblers. Poaching was one thing but risking a stray bullet entering a home and killing someone was an entirely different matter. Last deer season, a bullet had ripped through his house into his five-year-old daughter's room. It streaked over her bed into the adjacent bedroom where it bored into a dresser drawer and lodged inside a woolen blanket. Had his daughter been sitting up in bed, she would have been killed. His stomach wrenched at the thought. "We gotta get closer," he said. "It's not safe to shoot from here."

Jed knew about the incident. He wished he could have taken his words back as soon as he said them. He looked at Bo's face: chin thrust forward, temple pulsing. "You're, right," he said in a low voice. "Bad idea."

"I don't know what makes you so stupid, Jed, but it really works."

Jed shrugged off the comment, figuring he had it coming. "Those gobblers aren't gonna wait all morning. If we gotta get closer, let's do it."

Bo knew he was right. The birds could fly off at any minute. He dropped his pickup back into gear. "I'll try to pull alongside them for a clear shot. They look tame as chickens. Hopefully they won't take off."

Jed cracked open the rifle's bolt action just enough to check for a live round. He eased it back in place. "We're good to go."

Bo nodded and let the truck crawl forward until he came broadside to the birds. He stopped. Twenty yards of mowed grass separated him from his targets. He could've clobbered one with a stone. "Can't believe they never even looked up," he whispered. "Nice and slow now, hand me the rifle."

Bo eased open his door and slipped from the truck with his twenty-two. The turkeys pecked busily at their feed, each racing against the other in a frenzy to finish the grain. Choosing the fattest bird, he aimed carefully at its head and slowly pressed on the trigger.

KaPow!

A pink mist flew from the gobbler's skull, followed by bits of brain and bone. It dropped at once, its broad wings pumping futility against the ground. The others took flight immediately, gliding toward a distant woodlot like military choppers on a bombing raid.

Although it had been a small caliber bullet, the rifle's sharp report seemed especially loud in the valley surrounded by mountains, and both men knew the shot would alert anyone in the house. They had to move fast now. Jed swung open the passenger door and ran toward the turkey while Bo jumped back inside the truck and waited. Snatching the bird by its feet, Jed lifted it off the ground and raced back to the pickup. He opened the tool bin and tossed the turkey inside, slamming the lid. Its great wings fluttered against the aluminum walls as he pivoted on his feet—*How does that work when half your brains are gone?*—and ran to the front of the truck. He slid inside the cab and slammed the door. "Nice shooting, cuz," he breathed, puffing from exertion.

Bo nodded sharply and smiled. He decked the gas and raced toward the house, expecting to fly right past. But the lane only went a short distance beyond it before ending suddenly, cut off by a steep ravine. He slammed the brake. "I knew it!" he groaned. "I just knew things were going too good."

Jed turned and stared out the back window, eyes like saucers. "Bo! We gotta get out of here! Some old geezer just stepped out the door with a shotgun!"

With elbows flying, Bo jockeyed his pickup into an about-face. Foot pressed to the floor, he shot past Marcus Boggs in a boiling wake of dust, racing down the driveway until he reached the state road and turned onto it.

Jed's heart was pounding. "Think he got your license number?"

"Doubt it. I was almost airborne when I went by him. With all the dust he probably couldn't read it."

"Man, I hope you're right."

Bo looked at Jed, his face ashen. "Think he would have shot us?"

"I don't know. But I'm glad we didn't stick around to find out."

Minutes before the telephone rang, my wife and I had planned to head down town to celebrate our thirtieth wedding anniversary with dinner and a movie. It was three o'clock on Valentine's Day. And it was my day off.

"Sure you want to answer that?" she'd said, her tone sounding more like cautionary advice than a question.

I pretended not to notice. "It's probably just another road killed deer," I said, going for the phone.

It was a Sunday afternoon, in the middle of February. Hunting season had ended weeks ago. What could be happening? Really.

Even after twenty-five years on the job, I still found myself unable to ignore the Game Commission telephone when it rang. Like it possessed some weird gravitational force or something. I couldn't help but be drawn to it. Wyoming County—my assigned patrol area—held some of the most beautiful country in the state, and I felt like it all belonged to me personally.

I reached for the receiver and glanced at my wife, Mary Ann. A look of soft surrender played across her face. "Go ahead and get it," she sighed. "It'll just drive you crazy if you don't."

*P*oachers *always pick the most inconvenient times to do their dirty work,* I thought while turning the ignition in my patrol car. The incident had occurred less than thirty minutes ago. The complainant—a distraught Emma Boggs, I'd been informed by the dispatcher—had provided a vehicle description and a license number. After running the tag through PennDot, the dispatcher came up with an address on Township Road Ten. With any luck, the poachers would be there right now. I hoped to walk in on them, catch them red-handed.

After traveling ten miles, I turned onto the winding dirt road that would lead me to them and spotted a black Dodge pickup truck coming toward me. The driver looked right at me when he passed, eyes wide with surprise. I checked my side-view mirror. A large aluminum tool bin spanned the truck's bed, leaving little doubt that it belonged to one of the men I wanted. I flipped the switch on my red emergency light and cut a U-turn, thinking the chase was on. But the driver only went a short distance before drifting to the roadside where he came to a stop.

Maneuvering behind the truck, I remained aware of the inherent danger that all vehicle stops present to police officers. The suspect seated inside his vehicle cannot be readily seen. His back is toward you, hands undetectable, body shielded within a steel frame as you approach on foot. No matter how aware or how vigilant you may be, you remain a potential target. The most dangerous time comes as you step past the suspect's rear fender, your last possible cover. Nothing but open air separates you from the driver should he suddenly pull a gun.

Every police officer knows this. Every police officer risks his life, willingly, bravely, in every vehicle stop he makes. It comes with the job. It's what we do. And deep down inside, we know that sometimes the bad guy wins. He has the element of surprise on his side. And he often has nothing to lose. Many poachers are career criminals—losers with long rap sheets. Some are convicted felons who can't legally possess a firearm. One arrest away from a long prison term, they are desperate men. When faced with the possibility of incarceration, their desperation often breeds a reckless disregard of consequences as they consider their options toward the approaching officer.

As a result, enforcement officers are assaulted and sometimes killed when making even the most "routine" vehicle stops.

In order to best protect myself, I kept my vehicle's center in line with the suspect's left fender as I pulled behind it. This way, when I stepped out, I wouldn't be in a direct line with his door. It gave me cover, a place to hunker down should things go suddenly wrong. I watched the driver through his rear window and side-view mirror combined as I picked up my mike and radioed the license number along with my location. It only took a minute for the dispatcher to confirm that the tag came back clean from the National Crime Information Center and that there were no outstanding warrants.

I opened my door and walked toward the truck, glancing into the bed as I passed to make sure it was clear. I continued to watch the suspect as I approached, keeping close to the vehicle. He would have to do a one-eighty in his seat if he wanted me. From his side-view mirror, I could see both hands were gripping the steering wheel in a posture of submission. This he did purposely. It signaled that he was either a lawman or that he was streetwise. I was sure it was the latter.

Streetwise criminals are the most challenging outlaws a police officer can deal with. Not necessarily the most dangerous; however, they are shrewd and conniving individuals who often know basic law enforcement techniques and procedures better than some cops do. Wary that his submissive "hands up" display might be purely to lull me into complacency, I remained cautious. I stopped at the back edge of his door and peered into the open window.

"State Game Commission. I want to see some identification."

Bo's face was lined with dread as he dug a scruffy wallet from his back pocket. He pinched his driver's license between two filth-encrusted fingers and handed it out the window to me. He wore a brown Carhartt jacket and carpenter's jeans blotched with black car grease. Sandy hair grew long and thick over his collar. His eyes were brown, like stained walnut. According to his license, he was thirty-five, but he bore the look of a man ten years older.

"Guess you know why I stopped you," I said.

He cocked his head at squinted at me. "Not really."

"The turkey . . . ?"

"Turkey?" he said, feigning surprise. "What turkey?"

"The one that belongs to the tail feather I can see lying in the bed of your truck."

"In *my* truck?" He asked, shrugging a shoulder. "Gee, I guess it must've blew in there somehow."

"You think?"

Bo shook his head in rapid, woodpecker strokes.

I nodded at the back of his truck. "What about the blood on your tool bin? Wind do that too?"

Bo's smile began to slowly evaporate. His head sunk into his shoulders. "Okay. You got me," he sighed. "Don't know why I thought I could lie my way out of this."

"Happens a lot. I usually don't take it too personally."

"Thank you," he said.

"That is, as long as folks cooperate."

"Yes, sir." He offered a sheepish grin. "I ain't looking for more trouble."

"Good. I'd like to look inside your tool bin. Okay?"

"Yes, sir."

"But first I want you to get out of the truck and stand over by the tailgate."

Bo complied. After searching him for weapons, I climbed into the truck's bed and opened the tool bin. Along with an assortment of mechanic's tools, empty beer, cans and odd junk, I saw a rifle lying on a bloodstained, green trash bag stuffed half full. I picked up the gun, a bolt-action twenty-two, and opened the action. An empty casing popped out and spiraled to the floor. I picked it up and put it to my nose. It had been freshly fired.

"Who owns the rifle?"

Bo dropped his eyes and sighed in weary resignation. "I do."

I detached the fully loaded clip and pocketed it. "I'm guessing there's a turkey inside that plastic bag."

"Yes, sir," he said. Then he paused. "You . . . you aren't going to take my rifle, are you? It was my daddy's. I don't want to lose it."

"Depends on how much cooperating you do," I said. Opening the bag, I peeked inside and saw the entrails and feathered remains of a large turkey. "Where's the rest of it?"

"It's in Jed's oven," said Bo. "I just left his place."

"Jed . . . ?"

"My cousin."

Not wanting to walk into a house full of poachers without being prepared, I asked, "Who's there besides Jed?"

"Just him. He wanted to surprise his wife with a turkey dinner when she got home from work. It's Valentine's Day, you know. It's their anniversary."

I waggled my head in wonder. What were the odds?

"Should've taken her out for dinner and a movie," I said.

Bo nodded. "That's what *I* told him!"

"Then why this?" I asked, gesturing toward the bag of guts.

"Aw, Jed never listens to me. And he can't shoot worth a darn either. That's why I had to do it for him—why he talked me into going today. So he could say *he* killed it. Thought it would make him look macho or something."

How touching! A romantic poacher.

"Jed's always been able to make me do things," continued Bo. "We grew up together. When we was kids, he could talk me into just about anything: my favorite toy, my lunch money, you name it. Same when we was teenagers. Even talked me out of my girlfriend once. Then he took up with her."

"And you're still friends?"

Bo snorted. "Hard to believe. I know. I can't hardly believe it myself."

I couldn't help but feel sorry for the man. Apparently, his cousin had been leading him around his entire life.

"Okay, I've heard enough for now," I said. "I want you to head back to Jed's house. I'll be right behind you."

When we pulled into Jed's driveway, I kept a wary eye. I was in full uniform, driving a marked law enforcement vehicle. Although I considered it unlikely, the possibility of being ambushed by an irate poacher lingered in the back of my mind. There was no cover between my patrol car and Jed's house, only green grass. As in vehicle stops, the officer becomes an open target as he walks up to a suspect's home. So you stay on your toes, watch windows and doors during the approach.

I parked behind Bo's truck and had him accompany me to the house, a doublewide trailer that appeared well cared for. The curtained windows, painted exterior, and nicely landscaped shrubbery indicated that the occupants took pride in their possessions. It surprised me. I had expected to find a rundown trailer similar to the other homes I'd seen along the way.

We had taken but a few steps when the front door opened. A man walked out into the freezing cold wearing only jeans and a white cotton T-shirt. His hands stuffed deep into his pockets. "What's up?" he said offhandedly, as if a uniformed game warden escorting his cousin was no different than the mailman coming to the door with a package.

"I think you know what's up," I said.

He was tall, with dark, brooding eyes and a muscular build. He stopped in his tracks and stared at Bo critically.

Bo winced at him and shrugged. "Sorry Jed. He knows we did it. He saw blood on my truck and searched it. He took my rifle and said he'd keep it if I didn't cooperate. Looked inside the trash bag, too, Jed. He's got us cold."

"Your cousin is right," I said. "You might as well level with me. I know the turkey is in your oven right now. I have enough evidence to get a search warrant if I have to."

Jed eyed Bo briefly, then looked straight at me. "Okay," he said. "You're right. I'll be a man about it and admit it. C'mon in the house; it's cold out here and I'm freezing."

I nodded at Bo, signaling him to follow Jed while I trailed behind. The front door led directly into a warm and tidy kitchen, everything in its place. An adjacent living room looked neat and orderly with plush carpeting and well-placed, early American furniture throughout. I smelled the tantalizing aroma of a turkey roasting in the oven. My stomach growled. Jed must have heard it. He glanced over his shoulder at me. "Want something to eat?"

It had to be a joke, and it told me he'd accepted his fate and that he was simply trying to add some levity to the situation.

"No thanks," I said. "But it sure smells good."

"It's the bacon strips. Really adds to the flavor." He paused and turned to me. "Are you gonna take the turkey?"

I nodded. "It's contraband."

"Gonna eat it?"

"No. But I'll try to find a home for it."

Jed shrugged. "Long as it don't go to waste. Might as well take the pan, too. It's a throw-away." He glanced at Bo, then gave me a sheepish grin. "It was supposed to be a surprise for my wife. It's our anniversary."

I allowed an easy smile. "Aha."

A half-dozen biscuits lined the oven, ready to be popped in at a moment's notice. Jed bent over, opened the door, and pulled out an aluminum pan covered in foil paper. He carried it as gingerly as a newborn baby and set it on the counter. "Bummer, man. I was looking forward to a nice, turkey dinner. Anyway, it's been in for forty-five minutes. Two hours and fifteen to go for whoever gets it."

"I'll keep that in mind," I said. "Now, can we sit down? I have some paperwork to do."

He motioned toward the kitchen table. "Sure. Grab a chair."

I pulled out a chair and sat. Both men took seats directly across from me. They watched with interest as I jotted down

Jed's name and address on a consent-to-search form. I slid the document across the table along with a pen.

"This is the same as a search warrant," I said. "You can refuse to sign if you wish."

Jed's lips puckered into a huge frown. "What are you gonna do, search my house?"

"It's just for the turkey; that's all I'm going to take. Makes it legal."

He took the paper and studied it carefully before scribbling his name down and sliding it back to me. "How's that? No sense putting off the inevitable, I guess."

I folded the document and returned it to my jacket pocket. "I have another paper. One for each of you, actually. It's for your written confessions. You don't have to write a book, just jot down the details about how the turkey was killed, who shot it—that sort of thing."

I examined their faces. Both men looked at me with vacant stares. I took a blank form from my jacket and held it in my hand. "How about we start with you, Bo."

"Me?" There was genuine dread in his voice. "Gee, I don't know. I'm not much of a writer. Can't spell good either."

"No problem." I pushed the paper across the table at him. "Just do your best. A few sentences, that's all."

Bo looked like he'd just sucked a lemon. "It ain't gonna be pretty," he groaned. "But here goes . . ."

He scrawled his confession awkwardly, tongue playing peek-a-boo with his lips as he struggled with every written word. Watching him write was like watching someone carve his initials into tree bark with a dull pocketknife. After several long and tedious minutes, he finished. A gleam of sweat streaked his forehead as he handed his declaration to me and watched me look it over.

Jed saw turkees in the feeld. I drov my truck up too them and shot one. Then Jed ran and

got it. Later the game wardin came along and stoped me and he took my rifel away.

I folded the paper and tucked it back into my coat. "How about you, Jed?" I slid a blank confession form his way. "Take your time with it. Tell me everything you and Bo did."

Jed shrugged. "Not like I'll be telling anything you don't already know. Guess there's no sense lying about it."

Unlike Bo, Jed was more than comfortable with his penmanship. He took the paper and scribbled out a lengthy confession, detailing the entire incident step by step. But just as he handed the paper across the table to me, I heard a doorknob turn.

I looked up. The front door opened. A woman in her mid-thirties walked in. Blue eyes, blonde hair, well dressed . . . and utterly stunned by what she saw.

Jed swiveled in his seat. "Oh, hi honey," he said coolly. You would have thought she'd just walked in on a friendly poker game. "Have a little business to take care of. Done in a jiffy."

The woman stood frozen by the open door, eyeing me suspiciously. "Jed? What . . . what's going on?"

"Bo and me got into a little trouble with the law, that's all. Everything's gonna be okay. You'll see."

I watched her eyes drift toward Bo. She held him for a long moment.

Even talked me out of my girlfriend once . . .

"Hello, Bo," she said.

He glanced at me briefly before embracing her with his gaze. "Suzie," he said. "How are you?"

Jed cleared his throat, causing her to flash her eyes at him and turn toward the kitchen counter. "What's that in the pan?" she asked absently. "Are you making dinner, Jed?"

I stood from my chair. "State Game Commission, ma'am. I'm just finishing up my investigation. I'll have to take that with me. Sorry for the intrusion."

She lifted a corner off the covered bird. "A turkey!"

"It was gonna be a surprise, Suzie," Jed whined. "An anniversary surprise. Things sure have changed in a hurry."

She turned to her husband. "Oh, Jed, please! We could have just gone out for dinner. Maybe a movie afterwards. I really don't understand you sometimes."

Bo and I traded knowing glances, then looked away.

She turned toward me, eyes brimming with tears. "How much will the fine be, officer?"

"Two hundred dollars plus thirty-five in court costs. They'll likely have their hunting licenses revoked for a year or so, too."

She shook her head bitterly. "Hope you're happy, Jed." Then she turned and stormed from the kitchen into the bedroom, slamming the door behind her.

Jed exhaled an audible sigh. He studied the floor for a long moment before raising his chin, his face wretched with heartache. "The fine don't seem so bad compared to how much I hurt her," he breathed.

I picked up the turkey and started toward the door.

Glancing at Bo, I saw his face bore the same anguished expression as did his cousin. And I suspected, at least for the moment, they were both in love with the same woman.

M arcus Boggs smiled when he opened the door. It led directly into a warm and cozy kitchen. "Hello, warden," he said. "Did you catch those two bandits?" Well into his seventies, he was stoop-shouldered with silky, snow-white hair. His face covered with a day's worth of gray stubble.

"Yes, sir," I said. "You don't have to worry about them any more."

"Oh, I'm not worried about them at all," he said with a dry chuckle. "But they sure got my wife upset."

That makes two so far. And if I don't get home for our anniversary soon, mine will be number three.

"Marcus, who's there?" cried an elderly woman's voice. It came from the back of the house. "Who in the world are you talking to?"

Either Marcus didn't hear her or he didn't want to answer. Instead, he looked me in the eye and smiled mischievously. "I'm glad you got them; but to tell you the truth, I didn't know whether to chase those boys off or pin medals on their chests. I'm tired of buying feed for those fat-and-happy barnyard buzzards! My wife thinks they're her personal pets! Must be a hundred of 'em out there some days. Back's plumb wore out from hauling sacks of corn into the pasture."

"I appreciate that, sir. Mind if I ask you a question?"

He smiled at me with perfect teeth. "Why, sure, son. Go right ahead."

"They claim you came after them with a shotgun. Is that true?"

"Maaarrrrcuuus?" came the voice again. Louder this time and more insistent. "Who's out there with you?"

Again, Marcus didn't answer. "I was just trying to scare them, that's all. Worked too, didn't it?" He let out a jubilant cackle. "You should have seen them fly out of here!"

"I can imagine," I said. "Well, in that case, I guess I'll be on my way. I'd like to find someone who'll take the turkey before I get home; it's half cooked, and I don't want to see it go to waste."

Marcus Boggs rubbed his bewhiskered chin and offered a roguish grin. "You're looking at that someone right now."

I was taken aback. "Sure about that?"

Didn't he just tell me his wife thinks the turkeys are her personal pets?

"Sure I'm sure! I've been feeding them all winter long. Costs me a fortune, too. Why not have something good come out of it?"

I went to my patrol car, collected the turkey (still warm in the pan Jed had used) and brought it back to Mr. Boggs. It smelled wonderful as I walked into the kitchen and handed it to him.

"Perfect!" he said, beaming with delight. "Absolutely perfect. Thank you so much."

From around the corner, an elderly woman shuffled into the kitchen. She was bone thin with curled, gray-blue hair and what seemed a perpetual scowl.

Marcus Boggs winked at me. Then he tilted his head and whirled toward his wife with grand, theatric grace. "Emma, look!" he cried, arms outstretched. "Look what I have for dinner tonight!"

I stepped outside and closed the door behind me. And for a moment, questioned whether I'd detected an ornery edge in his voice or if his tone had merely been due to a state of heightened emotion as he presented the bird to his wife.

I guess I'll never know for sure. But considering it was Valentine's Day. A day that celebrates affection between couples. A day when gifts are exchanged by loved ones. I can only hope it was the latter of the two.

Fasten your seatbelts. It's going to be a bumpy night.
                              ~Joseph Leo Mankiewicz

Shadows in the Moonlight

IT **WAS LABOR DAY**, about ten p.m. when the phone rang. I snapped my eyes open. The TV was on, and Fox News anchor, John Gibson, was talking about the ongoing O. J. Simpson trial. My wife was curled up on the couch next to me. "No rest for the weary," she said as I rubbed the sleep from my eyes.

"How long have I been out?"

"About an hour."

I pushed myself up and hobbled toward the kitchen phone. Reports of night shooting had been on the increase in recent weeks. I expected trouble as I grabbed for the receiver.

The voice on the other end said a pickup truck had been spotlighting the fields along a rural road in the southeast corner of my district. Rifle shots were fired. He thought they'd killed at least one deer and worried that the recent upsurge in poaching would soon decimate the entire herd.

"Can you come out here right away?" he pleaded. "I live on Emerald Hill. You might catch them if you hurry."

I threw on my uniform and was driving east along Route Six within minutes. Pennsylvania remained in the death throes of a severe summer drought, and the warm, starry air promised more of the same. As I rocketed down the highway, my headlights often picked out the silhouettes of deer browsing near the berm. A common sight in Wyoming County, and for that matter, most of the state. Many had grown accustomed to traffic, making them easy targets for jacklighters as they foraged along the road's edge.

It would take twenty minutes to reach Emerald Hill. The poachers could be long gone by then. They'd have to suspect their gunshots would be heard. Although the area was rural, it wasn't devoid of people. Someone might call in the law.

But there remained a chance I'd still catch them. Meat shooters will often drop a deer and drive off, only to return hours later when they think it's safe. If I found a fresh carcass, I planned to conceal myself and wait for them. All night if need be.

But if they'd been drinking or were on drugs—or both, they might still be in the area. I hoped so. These are the lunatics who shoot at random, killing and wounding countless deer with no intention of retrieving a single carcass. For them, deer poaching is about target practice, not subsistence. Pop 'em and watch 'em drop. After a good night's shoot, I might find a dozen or more carcasses lying in open fields.

And then there are the horn hunters: Spineless cretins who drive through the veil of night searching for trophy bucks to shoot solely for their antlers. They leave the carcasses to bloat in the sun, brains oozing from ruptured skulls where antlers were hacked free. These are serious poachers. They don't shoot and run, only to come back later to claim their prize. Someone else might get there first—steal their horns. They are practiced butchers who can jump from a vehicle and skull-cap a buck in seconds. More than a few will be once-in-a-lifetime racks—trophy deer that the honest hunter never gets to see in the wild. But for the poacher, they are fond mementos. Illicit kills that only a warped mind can appreciate.

Too often, they're never caught. Occasionally, with good information or good luck—or both—on our side, we manage to apprehend them. These are the times when our job becomes most gratifying, for there's nothing like the heightened sense of accomplishment a game warden gets from stopping the indiscriminate slaughter of wildlife.

As I approached Emerald Hill, I dropped into a valley bordered by tall mountains, their velvet silhouettes surrounding me as I watched for the telltale sweep of a spotlight against the charcoal sky. It seemed the land had settled in for the night. Most folks had darkened their homes and gone to bed. There were no streetlights or lampposts here. The countryside dark and serene.

There was the sudden, fleeting swoop of a bat by my windshield. And as I watched it disappear into the moon shadow, the notion of recent gunfire seemed absurd. It would have been so out of place in the dreamy, sprawling landscape before me.

I turned onto an obscure back road and went several miles when I passed a pickup truck backed into the woods. Just off the road, it had been on my left, tucked under some pines. There were two figures sitting inside.

I brought my Bronco to a stiff halt and backed up, driving several car-lengths past the truck before stopping. Although I wasn't directly broadside to them, the maneuver still placed me in full view of my suspects. Approaching them head-on would be dangerous. Worse, my vehicle had created a rolling wave of dust that engulfed us in a thick, talc-like haze. Impossible to see, I grabbed my mike and called my location into headquarters along with a description of the truck. Then I waited for the fog to dispel before moving in.

The ensuing seconds became an eternity. Every active poacher—as I assumed these two might be—has at least one gun in his possession. Sitting in my vehicle, riding out the haze I'd created, made me a proverbial sitting duck. The skin on my back prickled as the dust began to settle around us.

As the mysterious truck started to materialize, I saw that both occupants were male. They sat woodenly in their seats. No furtive movements, no squirming or reaching around. This was good. All seemed well, at least for the moment.

My vehicle didn't have a mechanical spotlight, or I would have used it to temporarily blind the men. Instead, I eased open my door with my right hand while holding my flashlight in the other, keeping its beam trained on my suspects.

"State Game Commission!" I announced, moving toward them. Reaching their open window, I shined my light into the truck for a quick inspection. Both men had their hands on their laps, each with an open can of beer. The remains of two six-packs were scattered on the floor, but no guns or other weapons were apparent.

"What's this all about, officer?" the driver asked. Both suspects appeared intoxicated. The driver, perhaps, more so than his passenger.

"Do you have any firearms in the vehicle?" I asked.

"Nope!" said the driver. "We are unarmed."

I cast my light into the truck's bed for a moment. It was empty. "How long have you been here?"

The driver belched and wiped his mouth with a sleeve. "Long enough to finish most of the beer." He lifted his can and took a long drink, then he threw the empty on the floor with the others. "Got a couple left if you want to join us."

"I'd like to see some identification," I said.

The passenger peered at me through bleary eyes. "But we ain't done nothing wrong, officer."

"Appreciate that," I said. "And the sooner you show me some ID, the sooner we can part company."

Both men groped at their back pockets. I kept my light on their hands as they dug out driver's licenses and handed them to me.

Chester, the driver, was thirty-three but looked years older. He wore a Harley-Davidson baseball cap and thick round glasses. The address on his license showed that he lived a few miles away, in the next county. Ray, square jawed and clean shaven, was twenty-nine with a rural route address that indicated he lived nearby. Both men were dressed in jeans and plaid shirts.

I used my portable radio to inform the dispatcher that I had two white males stopped. I gave him their full names and birth dates. As a matter of routine, he would run the information through the National Crime Information Center (NCIC) to see if they had outstanding warrants. While waiting for an answer, I stepped back and took a closer inspection of the truck, looking for signs of deer hair or blood.

Convinced that the only thing they had killed tonight was a couple of six packs, I called dispatch to see if any information came back.

"Computer's down, Bill," came the reply. "You might have to wait awhile."

I've already wasted enough time with these two!

It was the last thing I wanted to hear.

"Ten-four, Dallas. I'm going to continue my patrol, but call me if anything comes back on them."

I said to Chester, "Plan on driving anywhere tonight?"

He stared at me with owlish eyes for a moment, then he blinked once and pointed a slender finger out the window. "See that house over there?"

Turning briefly, I observed a rundown, wood-sided dwelling on the opposite side of the road. "I see it."

"That's Ray's place. I'll be staying there. With him. All night."

"Good," I said, handing both men their licenses. "Because I don't think you're in any condition to drive."

I'd left them only minutes before, when my two-way radio came alive, the dispatcher informing me that Ray had outstanding warrants, and that the local constable wanted me to hold him until he got there.

I gunned the engine and circled back until I came to the dirt road where I'd first encountered the men. Turning in, I saw headlights coming toward me. Suspecting it was them, I stopped my vehicle in the road and stepped out.

I raised my hand, signaling the vehicle to stop. Chester's pickup truck eased alongside me and came to a halt. He peered out his open window at me, struck dumb by my presence.

"Shut the engine down," I said.

He complied.

"Hand me the keys."

He did.

"Where's Ray?"

He cocked his head back. "Just dropped him off at the house."

"I thought you were staying with him."

Chester looked like he'd just been caught stealing from the church basket. "Ah . . . I was going to but—"

A voice cut thickly through the dark: "But he changed his mind."

Ray!

He'd come from behind.

Caught off guard, I pivoted on my feet. Standing at the back of my vehicle, he began walking toward me.

I shined my flashlight in his face and palmed my gun. "Stop right there!"

He froze, shielding his eyes. "Hey!"

I lowered the beam to his chest, using my peripheral vision to observe Chester while Ray stood blinking at me.

"Ray, I want you to turn around and walk backwards toward me—Chester, keep your hands where I can see them and step out of the vehicle."

Chester balked. "I'm not gonna hurt—"

"Don't talk. Just do what I say."

Chester let out a nervous moan as he opened his door and stepped out. Ray, wobbly from too much beer, teetered backwards toward me as if he were negotiating an obstacle course. Fearing he'd fall and crack his head open, I moved to him and gripped the back of his collar with my left hand. "Don't turn; just walk with me, Ray."

I escorted both men into my headlights. Too drunk to out-maneuver me, I wasn't concerned about being attacked. But I still needed to frisk them for weapons. After separating the two, one on each side of the roadway, I handcuffed Ray and patted him down.

"Know why I'm back?" I asked.

"Yeah. I got warrants on me."

"That's right. You're under arrest; the constable is on his way." I sat him on the grass so he wouldn't trip over his own feet and hurt himself. Then, after administering sobriety tests on Chester—which he failed miserably—I radioed dispatch, informing them that I had Ray in custody and asked to have a state trooper come out for a DUI arrest on Chester.

Why are you here, man?" Ray was eyeing me in a peculiar way, as if I were some bizarre and grotesque zoo animal that had crawled from its den. "I mean . . . Chester and me . . . we were minding our own business, having a few beers. And then *you* come along."

The two men, both in handcuffs, sat in the grass near the edge of the lonely road. I sat in my patrol car with the door open, watching them. The troopers and the constable still miles away.

"Can you just tell me that?" whined Ray. "Why are you here? Nobody ever comes around here."

"I got a report about poaching," I said.

"Poaching!" he cackled. "Imagine that, Chester. He's here because of poaching!"

Chester dropped his head and waggled it. "Imagine that," he mimicked. "They've been poaching around here for years and we never see a game warden. Now, when nobody's doing anything wrong, the man in green shows up. Imagine that, Ray."

Ray snickered drunkenly. "Poachers! What a joke! I'll tell you what *I* always say, buck or doe, down they go!"

Chester said, "Why don't you shut up, Ray? We're already in enough trouble."

Ray said, "Buck or doe, down they go; buck or doe, down the go . . ."

Chester shouted. "Shut up, Ray!"

"Knock it off. Both of you," I snapped. I turned to Ray. "The fine for deer poaching is five hundred dollars for each animal. It can get a lot higher, too."

"Five hundred! Is that right? Whew! A deer ain't worth five hundred dollars."

"Good reason not to poach one." I said.

Ray scoffed. "Good reason not to get caught, you mean."

A smart aleck. No surprise he'd been arrested before "What are your warrants for?" I asked.

Ray regarded me for a moment. "They ain't for poaching," he snorted. "I'll tell you that. And you'll never catch me, either. Had a good teacher: my daddy."

"I'm sure he's proud."

Ray sneered at me. "Not any more. He's dead!"

I regretted my remark. My own mother had passed away not long ago. "Sorry about your father," I said.

Ray cocked his head. "You ain't so bad, you know? I kinda like you! And here I thought all lawmen were jackasses!" He raised his cuffed hands. "Appreciate you not jacking these too tight like some of the others. Anyway, my warrants are for driving under suspension and disorderly conduct, since you asked."

"Suspension for what?"

He heaved a weary sigh. "Driving under the influence," he said, spelling it: D . . . U . . . I."

This was Chester: "Imagine that, Ray. You're being arrested for warrants, and I'm being arrested for drinking, all because some idiot called about a poacher!"

Ray nodded glumly. "Imagine that."

Chester looked at me and said, "Thanks a lot for ruining my life, mister. I drive for a living. If I lose my license, I lose my job. So . . . thanks a lot for ruining my life."

He sat on his inebriated rump, sulking. As if circumstances beyond his control had caused him to drink and drive. I wasn't surprised. In the outlaw universe, someone other than themselves is always responsible for anything bad that happens to them. Tonight it was my fault.

"Chester, you were responsible for your own actions," I said. "Not me."

Chester sat elbows on knees, holding his head in his hands. "Well," he muttered, "all I know is . . . thanks a lot for ruining my life."

In a way, I couldn't help but feel sorry for the fellow. And for a moment, considered releasing him from custody so long as he promised to stay at Ray's house tonight. But he had lied to me before. I couldn't trust him. If he were to drive off and kill somebody, I'd never forgive myself.

"Chester?" I said.

He raised his head and blinked at me with sad, rheumy eyes.

"Did you ever consider that I might be *saving* your life instead of ruining it?"

"Huh?"

"Sometimes the lessons hardest learned are the most beneficial," I said.

Chester wrinkled his face into a deep frown. "Lesson? I don't need a lesson, I need a cigarette. Got any?"

I shook my head and reached for my portable. Dispatch was trying to contact me. I keyed the mike. "Go ahead, Dallas."

"Just heard from PSP; their ETA is thirty minutes. The constable is right behind them, too. Your driver has prior DUI arrests, Bill. They're pretty familiar with the guy."

Thirty minutes will be an eternity with these two, I thought. All I wanted was to get back in my vehicle and go. My deputy was expecting me for a few hours of night patrol, and he lived clear on the other side of the county.

Chester looked up at me. "They'll lock me up and throw away the key this time," he said. "Thanks a lot, warden. Thanks a lot for ruining my life." Then he hung his weary head and continued to mutter those same words over and over again, until finally, exhausted, he settled down in the cool grass and fell fast asleep.

The night so clear, we could see clean into the next county, Deputy Gene Gaydos and I parked on a hilltop and waited for a light to arc across the indigo skyline. It was one o'clock in the morning. Below us, a series of narrow dirt roads sliced through the remote landscape. Spotlighting was illegal after midnight. And at a lofty one thousand feet, we'd be sure to see the telltale beam of any jacklighter who might be operating in the sprawling darkness below.

The air was soft and warm and smelled of freshly mowed hay as it breezed through my open window. In the moonlight, I saw a red fox hunting the field to my left, a large white tip on its bushy tail. So close I could almost touch it, the fox paid no mind to my vehicle as it padded through the low grass with its nose to the ground. It stopped suddenly and curled its back catlike, body taut, motionless. Then, quick as lightning it pounced. There was a muffled squeak. A hapless field mouse. Pinning it with both paws, the fox brought its head down and flipped the rodent into the air. Snatching it in its mouth, it chewed greedily, tiny bones crunching like peanut brittle as the fox devoured its prey with cheerful indifference.

"See that!" I whispered.

Gaydos nodded. "He'll get a bellyful tonight. Alfalfa's just been cut; makes them easier to catch."

"At least we have some entertainment. Sure is quiet."

"Bars close at two. Things might pick up then."

I grabbed my thermos and turned the rubber stopper. It squeaked, then opened with a hollow *thunk!* The fox cocked its head and stared, wondering, perhaps, if I'd caught a mouse of my own. I chuckled softly and poured. As the steaming coffee gurgled into my cup, the fox turned and continued its hunt.

"Donut?" I asked, reaching for the bag.

"No thanks. I packed something."

"Sure? They're custard. My favorite."

Gaydos shrugged. Not interested

I quickly polished off the treat and wiped my mouth with a napkin. "What did you bring?"

"Carrot sticks and celery."

I shook my head in mock sympathy. "Betcha can't wait to dig in, huh?"

Gaydos rolled his eyes at me. "You are what you eat, Bill."

I closed the bag of donuts and sipped my cup. The fox zigzagged across the open meadow to my left, its sleek fur glistening silver under the moonlight. In the distance, the haunting call of a great horned owl filled the night: *Hoo-hoo-hoooo hoo-hoo!* It gave me a sensation of tranquility and peace, and I eased back in my seat to listen.

Suddenly two muffled gunshots echoed across the hills. I jolted erect and stared into the windshield. "Where'd *that* come from?"

"Behind us, Bill." Gaydos was buckling his seat belt. "Maybe a half mile, no more than that." He looked at me and wrinkled his brow. "You okay?"

"Just a little coffee," I said, blotting my shirt with a napkin.

Gaydos didn't acknowledge. "They're shooting by moonlight, too. No light. They're not amateurs."

I capped my thermos, keyed the ignition, and started down the mountain road with my lights out. My Bronco was equipped with a homemade cutoff switch for the rear, so I didn't have to worry about a red flash giving me away when I applied the brakes. The one thing I did worry about, however, was running into a poacher (literally) who happened to have the same idea. I moved completely in the dark. My eyes strained into the roadway as I steered through the curves while Deputy Gaydos watched the distant landscape for suspicious vehicles. If we spotted one, I'd pull right up to the back bumper. Then it would be headlights, red lights, and a *whoop!* from my siren for good measure. I used this method whenever possible to avoid high-speed chases. The visual impact of a well-lit police vehicle on their tail from out of nowhere usually stopped them cold. If they saw me coming from a distance, they'd run for certain, their wheels kicking up a choking storm of dust, making it impossible to tail them without risking a crash.

As we moved along, we came upon an occasional home tucked into the remote valley below. The possibility that an individual may have stepped out the back door to shoot a deer, lingered in my mind. I slowed to a crawl while Gaydos watched for someone dragging a carcass. But sound travels in the country, especially at night. My approaching vehicle could be heard for a long way off. Anyone on foot would have plenty of time to duck for cover.

I often wondered how many deer in Pennsylvania were shot illegally from open windows and doorways throughout the course of a year. Thousands, I suspected. Unless a neighbor reports the violation, and a game warden shows up with a search warrant, most of these poachers are never caught. Like tonight, even though my deputy and I were in the immediate area when the shots were fired, the odds of catching a backyard poacher were almost nil. And as we made our way along one back road after another, with no sign of a vehicle, we came to realize that our effort was in vain.

T hat makes two times tonight!" I grumbled.

"Not your fault," said Gaydos. "We only get the dummies on night patrol; you know that."

"It still bothers me."

"If it wasn't for dimwits with spotlights and high-powered rifles telling us where they are, we'd hardly catch anybody at all."

I rolled down my window, eyes scanning the grassy meadow for the fox. He was long gone. In the distance, a radio tower twinkled intermittently. The night had turned eerily still.

"Anyone could hit a deer without a spotlight tonight," I said. "You can see clearly for a good hundred yards, the moon is so bright. I think that's what just happened. Someone is home right now, cutting up an illegal deer, and there's not a thing we can do about it."

Gaydos grunted in agreement.

"The really smart ones are using crossbows or rifles with silencers," I declared. "All you need for a homemade silencer is a hacksaw, some aluminum pipe, and a sponge to insulate it with."

"Or a tin can, or a plastic bottle," added Gaydos.

"Crossbows are selling like crazy these days," I said. "The perfect weapon for poaching. They're accurate, extremely deadly and—

"—Hey! There's a light!"

A bright yellow shaft arced across the sky and then quickly went out. Someone was working a spotlight in the fields below us. The fact that it blinked out so fast meant it probably came from a moving vehicle. Poachers will often shine a field until a house or a barn appears. Then they arc the beam up and across the sky to avoid hitting it. The last thing they want, is to light up someone's home and alert the occupants.

"They're in Sugar Hollow," Gaydos said, fastening his seatbelt. "Could be any of a number of roads, but they're in the hollow for sure."

I started the engine, dropped the Bronco in gear, and stomped the accelerator. At the first curve, I reached down and turned on my headlights. "No sense killing ourselves before we catch up to them."

Gaydos shook his head and mouthed something. It looked like, *Thank God!*

I breezed down the Mountain and turned right on the macadam road. It was a narrow, winding, two-lane highway with many sharp curves. No way I could make good time, but I pushed my vehicle to the limit without being reckless. Soon the terrain dropped into a broad valley to our right, giving us an opportunity to see for a considerable distance.

"There!" said Gaydos suddenly. "We just passed them!"

I saw it too. But only for a second as I rounded a quick bend. A pickup truck with yellow clearance lights dotting the roof. It was cruising slowly down the center of an obscure dirt road.

I screeched to a grinding halt and backed up until I reached the road. I quickly turned in. The truck was gone! Dust from its fleeing wheels hung in the air like an oppressive fog.

"They must have seen us coming," I said. My eyes were glued to the road as I gobbled up the distance. I could barely see twenty feet in front of me.

"It's a dead end road, Bill. They've got no place to go."

Suddenly, twin high-beams loomed through the haze. Above them, a telltale row of yellow clearance lights.

Our suspect had turned around and was boring toward us at a deadly pace.

I switched on my revolving red light, thinking it might stop him. But the lunatic truck shot by my vehicle, taking my side mirror with it.

My elbows pumped like a boxer working a heavy bag as I brought my vehicle to an about-face. But as I swung around to go after them, the front end dropped into a drainage ditch. I felt the frame hit with a sickening thud. It was bad.

I shifted into reverse and tromped on the gas, hoping to muscle out. My rear wheels smoked like a top fuel dragster at the spring nationals, but the Bronco wouldn't budge. Valuable seconds raced by. I jerked the floor lever into four-wheel drive and slammed my foot on the accelerator.

The front wheels dug in, and we bounced from the trench and came down with a spine-jarring thud. We flew backwards so fast that my rear wheels dropped off the opposite bank before I could stop. Stuck again, I gunned the engine and clawed my way back onto the road. A mix of mud and stones exploded from my tires. Hopes of catching the fleeing truck were dwindling fast. I slammed the accelerator and shot forward, reaching the hard road in less than a minute.

"Go right!" barked Gaydos. "They'll be heading for the highway!"

I cut my wheels and burned onto the macadam road. Red light arcing into the night. Siren at full wail, I went as fast as conditions would allow, but by the time I reached the state highway, the truck was gone.

Deputy Gene Gaydos and I were parked high on our overlook, reflecting upon the lousy night we were having, my mood growing more somber by the minute. Three times I had chased after suspected poachers; they'd managed to elude me on each occasion.

Blind luck and circumstance generally dictates success or failure on most night patrols. Unfortunately, tonight our luck had been all bad. But that isn't always the case. Many times, I'd come upon a poaching incident on some remote road to nowhere for no other reason than making a whimsical left turn instead of a right. After all, most game wardens spend half their working lives driving aimlessly through backcountry without a fixed direction or final destination. It's called routine patrol, and we manage to stumble into our fair share of poachers that way.

But our best cases are usually obtained through information received from civilian witnesses. Be it a next-door neighbor, a jilted girlfriend, or somebody out walking a dog. The eyes and ears of the public have always been the law enforcement officer's best friend.

Which is why I always strived for a reputation as firm but fair. A game warden with a bad name or insulting demeanor is his own worst enemy. Nobody wants to associate with an arrogant officer. In rural counties your reputation is made—or unmade, in short order. If folks learn to trust you and believe in you, they are much more likely to call when they see a violation.

Early in my career, I started writing a weekly wildlife column for the local newspaper. I also did a live radio program each week called *The Wyoming County Sportsman*. Both avenues enabled me to reach out to the public. People who never met me personally got to know me pretty well by reading the articles I wrote or listening to my weekly broadcasts about the Game Commission. As a result, they were more inclined to approach me with information on illegal hunting activity.

But tonight, catching bad guys was a product of pure happenstance. We knew the county had been plagued with poaching activity for years. And the hill we chose to watch over the descending landscape, proved ideal for covert surveillance. But the rest was all hit and miss—mostly miss as it turned out so far.

Although it was approaching three o'clock in the morning, I wasn't ready to pack it in, so I rolled down my window, settled into a comfortable position, and reached for my Stanley thermos.

"Want some coffee?" I asked Gaydos.

"I brought tea."

"Must really hit the spot with the veggies, huh?"

He knew I was teasing and ignored me.

I twirled the cap off my thermos and pulled the rubber stopper. It made a moist popping sound. Steam from the hot coffee curled lazily toward the Bronco's roof. I poured, breathing in the fresh aroma.

"Nothing like the smell of black coffee when you're on night patrol," I declared. "Donut, Gene?"

"No thanks."

I ran my fingers across the floor behind me until I found the bag. "Ah!"

Gaydos stared out the windshield, watching for another spotlight.

"Enough for both of us," I said, digging into the bag. "Sure you don't want one?"

He reached down and pulled a black construction worker's lunch box from between his feet. "I'm sure. Judy packed a lunch for me." He placed the pail on his lap and unsnapped the stainless steel latch. "Two sandwiches here," he offered, opening the lid.

"No thanks," I said, chomping on my donut. "I'm good."

I was about to pour more coffee when I noticed Gene having difficulty with his thermos. I watched him struggle from the corner of my eye. He had a death grip on the rubber stopper and was trying with all his might to twist if off. After several hearty attempts, he sat back and heaved a long sigh.

"Can't open it?" I asked.

"I'll get it. My hand keeps slipping."

He held the thermos firmly on the seat. Squeezing it with his thighs for good measure, he grasped the stopper and twisted, his face turning beet red as he gave the maddening plug one last opportunity to comply. "Good grief!" he said in a final breath of frustration.

"Want me to try?"

"Nope! I can get it." Gaydos was aware of my background as a former bodybuilding champion and knew I could still bench press three hundred pounds on a good day. The last thing he wanted was for me to muscle it open with one twist and then tease him about it for the rest of his days.

He knew me well.

"Why are you shaking your hand?" I asked. "Hurt yourself?"

"It's like Judy used a wrench when she tightened the stopper," he groaned. "I almost dislocated my wrist."

"That's your gun hand, too," I cautioned, reaching for the thermos. "You still might have to save my life tonight."

Gaydos looked at his throbbing hand and let out a submissive sigh. He gave the thermos to me. "Go ahead. Give it a try."

Eyeing him with a predatory grin, I took a deep breath and grasped the rubber stopper. Then, with a sudden and explosive burst, I wrenched against it with all my might, fully expecting it to pop right off.

When it didn't budge, I sucked in another gulp of air and quickly shifted hands. I twisted on the stubborn plug until my head wanted to explode. Finally, heaving from exertion, I stared at my deputy in bewilderment. "Wow! Judy must have some grip!"

Gaydos regarded me for a moment. Then his face began to twitch with amusement.

"What?" I said. Then, after a pause, "You knew I wouldn't do it, didn't you?"

He let out a soft chuckle. "It's vapor locked, Bill. The last time it happened I had to use a strap wrench to get it off. And it was still a struggle.

"Vapor locked?"

"Yes," he explained. "It was filled with hot tea hours ago. The liquid has cooled since then, creating a vacuum that sucked in the stopper tight enough to store nuclear waste inside."

Gaydos broke into laughter, which started me laughing too. I was glad for it. The incident helped lighten our sour moods over the terrible luck we'd been having tonight.

"Speaking of nuclear waste," I chuckled, "you're welcome to some of my coffee."

Suddenly a shot rang out in the valley below us. Gaydos slammed his lunch pail shut and snapped on his seat belt. "Look! There's the light!"

"Hold tight!" I cried. "This time they're not getting away!"

And with that, we rocketed down the lonely mountain road in a storm of brown dust.

Bears when first born are shapeless masses of flesh a little larger than mice, their claws alone being prominent. The mother then licks them gradually into proper shape.
~Pliny the Elder
A.D. 23 – 79

A Reckoning in the Snow

DEPUTY ZIKA EASED his vehicle along the snowy township road and scanned the rolling, white countryside. Several large bears had been sighted in North Branch Township near the Wyoming County line, one of them rumored to weigh over five hundred pounds. Zika suspected that the prospects of killing this trophy black bear, coupled with the light tracking snow from the night before, would create some serious hunting pressure in the area.

This was a time when Pennsylvania had a statewide bear season that ran for three days—Monday through Wednesday—with no provision in the law for an extension. The annual kill was often defined by the weather. An early sustained cold snap or heavy snowstorm would induce many bears to den too soon, bringing dismal prospects for hunters who had waited all year for the season to arrive.

But this year the weather forecast couldn't be better. The entire week predicted to be in the low thirties with a light snowfall each day. Cool temperatures, combined with a daily tracking powder, would keep hunters pushing hard. The bear population was at a peak. Zika had been getting complaints about nuisance bears all summer long due to last season's poor kill when deep snows had shut down mountain roads, making foot travel all but impossible.

Last year's lost season brought hunters out in droves today. Zika saw cars and trucks pulled off the road wherever they found room. Foot trails broke through the snow in every direction, crossing into the surrounding woodlands and hollows like spokes on a wheel. In the distance, he heard the raucous clang of pots and pans mixed with wild hoots and hollers. A hunting party putting on a drive. He wished them luck. Fewer bears wreaking havoc with farm crops and neighborhood garbage cans would certainly be a blessing.

Zika continued across the county line (indicated by a metal road sign—pockmarked by shotgun pellets—that said *Bradford County*) and made a U-turn in the road between two farms. Both contained freshly painted, red barns sitting amid sprawling horse pastures. These were once owned by hard working dairy farmers who sold out to folks with real money from New Jersey and New York. The land had been open to hunting before, but the new owners were city folks who posted their property with "No Trespassing" signs. From the barn nearest Zika, a man stepped outside and waved at him frantically.

Thinking there was a hunting violation, he steered down a long driveway to the barn and exited his patrol car.

"Good morning, sir," the deputy said.

"It was until all the shooting started," the man scoffed. "I moved into the country for peace and quiet; now I have to put up with this nonsense. Sounds like a war zone back there! What's everyone hunting for, anyway?"

"Bear season opened today," said Zika. "That's a pretty big deal around here."

"Bear season? Good! The scent of a bear spooks my horses. Hope they kill them all!"

"I doubt they will, sir," said Zika. "But if your land wasn't posted they might have a better chance at it."

He fixed the deputy with an incredulous stare. "You can't be serious!"

"Just a thought."

"I own stallions worth more than you make in a year! I can't allow a bunch of imbeciles with guns on my property. What if they shoot a horse?"

Zika could see he was wasting his time. "I understand, sir. Now, if there's nothing else, I'll have to be on my way."

The horseman nodded firmly. "Understood. You have a job to do. Go on, then."

Zika started toward his patrol car, then paused and did an about-face. "You said you heard shooting?"

He raised a gloved hand and pointed. "Right back where you just came from, deputy. About thirty minutes ago, in the woods bordering the road there."

Two hunters trudged across the snowfield a hundred yards from his vehicle. Both dressed in camo-orange, they leaned forward as they pulled small bears by ropes at their necks. They had come from the woods where the horseman had heard all the shooting and were heading toward a pickup truck parked by the road.

Zika raised his field glasses and focused on them. One an adult, the other a youngster. He walked in awkward, choppy steps, struggling to keep up. Suspecting they were father and son, he looked forward to congratulating the boy on what might be his very first bear. He parked behind their vehicle and waited.

But as the two figures came close, the taller one paused to stare at his patrol car. Then he turned and looked back, waiting until the boy caught up. They faced each other there, deep in conversation, the boy glancing toward the deputy, then quickly back at the woods.

His presence obviously concerned them. But why? Were the bears untagged? Or was there something in the woods they didn't want him to see? Illegal bait, perhaps?

Zika donned his badged Stetson and strode to the field's edge. He waved at the hunters to signal them in. They waved back immediately, then dropped their chests and plodded toward him like condemned men headed for the gallows. Their body language spoke volumes. Something was definitely wrong.

"State Game Commission," said Zika as the hunters approached. "Looks like you've both had a pretty good morning."

"Lucky," said the elder. A golf ball sized wad of tobacco bulged in his cheek. He was in his mid-thirties with about a week's growth of stubble. Generous shocks of sandy hair pushed out from under a bright orange hunting cap.

"This young fella your son?" asked Zika.

The man put a hand on the boy's shoulder. "Yup."

He was in his early teens. Zika smiled. "Congratulations on the bear!"

The young man dropped his chin, his face exuding a silent resentment.

And the deputy knew.

"How old are you, son?" asked Zika.

He answered—"Fourteen"—without looking up.

"This your first bear?"

"Yessir."

Zika turned to his father, disgusted by what he saw. But he chose not to embarrass the boy any further by interrogating either of them. Instead, he said, "You must be proud of your son, taking a bear so early on the first day."

The man grinned. "He's quite the hunter all right! Just like his old man. Been going out with me since he was five."

"Taught him everything you know, huh?"

"Guess I did, warden." He spat a stream of brown goo into the snow. "We got proper licenses. Want to see them?"

Zika took their hunting licenses, along with the elder's driver's license, back to his patrol car. He transferred the information onto a Field Information Report. Then he examined both bears. They were male cubs weighing about seventy pounds. Both were legally tagged but hadn't been gutted, indicating the hunters were in a hurry to leave.

The season limit was one bear per hunter. Because he lacked evidence of a violation, Zika let them go. He was certain the father had killed both bears, the boy's sullen demeanor proof alone. As a deputy for more than twenty years, he'd met hundreds of youngsters with their first deer or bear—or for that matter, first anything: squirrel, rabbit, pheasant—you name it. The one thing they all had in common was an expression of satisfaction and joy—a sense of accomplishment that shone on their faces. He'd also met youngsters who were robbed of the thrill of the hunt when someone did the shooting for them. They too had something written on their faces: disappointment and regret. In rankled him every time he saw it.

And he recognized it today in the boy's dark eyes.

As he backtracked their zigzagging trail, west through the woods, Zika learned they had dragged the bears over rough terrain for a quarter mile until finally reaching the field where he first saw them. It would have been much easier to go in a southerly direction a mere one hundred yards to the road. It ran parallel to the woods, and junior could have waited there with the carcasses while dad walked back for the truck, thereby avoiding an hour of backbreaking labor.

So, why the hard way? The only logical reason, he knew, was because they didn't want to be seen near the kill site he'd just come upon. Here a large crimson bloom stained the snow. Blood. And there was something else. Something that made his jaw tighten as he approached.

Lying at the base of a towering pine, he saw the bloody carcass of a third cub. Shot multiple times, it had been left behind like a cheap, discarded ragdoll.

Zika stepped back. He did not want to interfere with the crime scene. Years on the job made him treat every investigation as a prospective court case. Although there was no doubt in his mind that the two he'd checked earlier were responsible, it would take more than speculation to convict them if the case went to trial. From this point on, the cub's unlawful killing would be pursued with the same passion and intensity as a murder case. More officers would be called in, the vicinity scoured for promising leads, with every piece of evidence collected and preserved.

Deputy Zika reached for his handheld radio and called for backup.

When Bundy grabbed my mike, he came dreadfully close to being coldcocked by a wild right elbow. We were driving up Forkston Mountain on a precarious two-track. I had miscalculated. What started as light snow-powder had suddenly turned the road into a frozen snowpack. My elbows whirled in a blur of motion as I whipped my steering wheel left and right to keep from veering into oblivion.

Below us was a sheer precipice one thousand feet deep. I got airsick every time I glanced over. We could only go up. Backing down was not an option. It would mean using my brakes. Impossible. We'd slide right off the rim!

Bundy brought my mike to his face. "Five-three-eight by; go ahead with your message."

I heard Deputy Zika call for assistance with an illegal bear kill. I wondered if we'd live long enough to get there.

Bundy was more confident, "Ten-four," he said. "We're tied up; be there as soon as we can."

I had managed to make it halfway up the mountain, praying all the while that no other vehicles came down the other way. We'd be at an impasse. Stuck bumper to bumper, I guessed, until spring. That or we'd need a helicopter to lift us off the narrow trail. Really. It was that bad.

"Roll down your window," I barked, cranking my own down. "It's getting hot in here!" I was sweating like a marathoner in a July heat wave. Every muscle in my body tense. Thrill seekers in their snowmobiles had compacted the snow-covered road into a frozen bobsled trail that twisted and turned at every opportunity. And at each curve, I wondered if one of them would come crashing around the bend at us.

I didn't expect this; but it was no excuse. I never should have gone up, knowing we had snow on the road. I didn't have chains with me either, and I was astonished that my Bronco could ascend the treacherous road so well. It reminded me of the indestructible fifty-three Willys Jeep I once owned. The little four-wheeler could go just about anywhere and often managed to get me into the same trouble I found myself wallowing in today.

I hollered at Bundy over the harsh grate of my tires grinding into the snow crust. "Once we get to the top (trying to sound positive here), we can head down the opposite side. It'll be the south face. Hopefully, not as icy."

Bundy quickly gripped his armrest for support as my tail end slid toward the cliff's edge. My heart leaped, thinking we'd go over. But the tires suddenly took hold, propelling us forward once again.

"Close one!" I cried. "We're halfway to the top!"

Bundy offered a supportive smile. "We'll get there, Bill. You're doing fine!"

He had more faith in me than I had in myself. Larry Bundy worked for the state Fish & Boat Commission as a Waterways Conservation Officer. Pennsylvania, unlike other states, has two separate wildlife agencies overseeing its natural resources. Waterways officers are charged with managing aquatic habitat and enforcing fishing and boating regulations, while game officers are responsible for managing wild birds and mammals as well as enforcing hunting and trapping regulations. Although we are assigned separate jurisdictions, officers from either agency have overlapping powers to enforce natural resource laws throughout the Commonwealth. Bundy was in his "off-season" and wanted to spend the day with me.

I wondered if he regretted it.

The mighty Ford Bronco continued to claw its way upward, tires spinning and then grabbing hold to boost us another ten or twenty yards closer to the top. It was a long and exhausting journey, but after thirty minutes wrestling with my steering wheel, I rounded a sharp bend and saw open sky. A sense of relief came over me. Just ahead, lay one final steep bench to the top. With my foot steady on the gas so we wouldn't spin out, I chugged upward inch by inch until my patrol car flattened out on a broad plateau of birch and oak. I stopped and slumped back into the seat. "Thank God!" I breathed. "We finally made it."

Bundy chuckled. "A lot of people would pay good money for a thrill ride like that."

"Don't know about them, but I just aged ten years."

"I hope the other side looks better. Zika sounded like he had something interesting."

I dropped the Bronco into gear and started across the level plateau. "If it's anything like what we've just seen, we'll need chains to get down. There are a few camps up here. Maybe someone has a set we could borrow."

"I think they might," said Bundy.

He was being diplomatic, of course. Only a fool would come up here without chains. Mine were lying in a pile in the garage where I'd left them since last year. Hunting season had kept me hustling for weeks on end. As a result, I'd forgotten to throw them in my vehicle at the first sign of bad weather.

I continued across the flat for a half mile until the road disappeared down the south face. Bundy and I exited my Bronco and started exploring the passage on foot before attempting a descent. As difficult as our climb had been up the north face, we realized it would be much worse going downhill if icy conditions prevailed. Your brakes are the enemy on a slippery surface—and it would be impossible not to use them on the steep grade ahead. But since this had been the first snow of the season—a relatively light three inches—we hoped that the road on the sunnier, southern side of the mountain would be clear.

And to our combined delight, only the first hundred feet retained snow, loose and melting into the muddy two-track. Hastening to assist Deputy Zika with his bear case, we clambered back up the grade and jumped into the Bronco.

"There'll be some slippery spots on the way down," I said. "We ain't home yet."

"It can't be any worse than what we just went through," said Bundy, his tone optimistic.

"You're right," I said, slipping the Bronco into low range. "I'm gonna make this baby walk to the bottom like a six-legged mountain goat."

My vehicle was equipped with all-terrain tires for maximum traction. They kept the rig steady while the four-wheel-drive system allowed me to creep down the slick and twisting two-track without using my brakes. In less than a half-hour, we had wormed our way to the bottom and leveled out. But as we made our way to the state highway, we were forced to stop at a wooden bridge. Slim and rickety, it spanned a small but steep creek bank. Because we were in a hollow shaded by tall pines, the terrain here remained snow-covered.

I stepped out to inspect the bridge, walking forty feet to the other side and then back again. Constructed of heavy wooden planks, the old and weathered structure had no guardrail to protect us from a twenty-foot drop into the frigid mountain stream. To make matters worse, the snowpack remained partially frozen. The entire span barely wide enough for my tires, one tiny miscalculation could send us plummeting off the edge.

I stood at the edge and envisioned myself trapped upside-down in the creek below, icy water pouring into the windows while I struggled to free myself. But with no choice but to risk crossing or be marooned till spring, I climbed back into my Bronco and started driving across the narrow overpass.

When I reached the middle, wheels inching forward, all I could see out my side window was blue sky. I was a man on a tightrope. I kept my eyes dead ahead. Prayed my wheels wouldn't veer. Ahead, the snow-covered bridge melted into the white landscape, only adding to the unsettling sensation of floating in midair.

Without warning, my front end slid to the right. My heart exploded as I felt a wheel drop off the edge. I sucked a deep breath and stomped the brakes, knobby tires clawing into the frozen crust like grappling hooks. Certain we were going over, my eyes locked on the frozen creek below, anticipating the crushing impact that would soon come.

Then, just as suddenly, we stopped. I stared out the windshield. Looking down, it might as well have been the Grand Canyon. Praying we wouldn't slide any further and fall into a sudden nosedive, I slipped the gearshift into park. Then I set the emergency brake and shut down the engine. "How close to the edge are we?"

Bundy rolled down his window and hung his upper body out. He looked straight down, then swiveled his head left and right. "Your front tire is hanging in midair, Bill." He fell back into his seat and turned toward me, his expression bleak. "Your back tire is sitting right on the edge."

I swallowed hard. "Man, that's not good."

Bundy nodded.

I pushed open my door and stepped out. "Let's take a look at the damages."

We had only a foot-wide portion of the bridge to walk on. The Bronco took up the remaining share. Bundy and I sidestepped along the snow-covered catwalk until we cleared the Bronco's rear fender and could move about on the bridge for a better look. Dropping on our bellies, we peeked under the chassis. Both wheels on the driver's side rested on solid snowpack, giving us hope we could still pull free. But we had come to a stop parallel with the bridge, the right front wheel dangling helplessly off the edge, while the rear wheel rested dead even with the bridge's outer rim, the rubber so close to the brink it seemed all I need do was give the Bronco a casual bump and it would topple right over.

We stood to our feet and faced each other. "No sense both of us getting killed," I said. "It only takes one to drive this rig. Besides, I'm going to need you to guide me forward once I break free."

Bundy regarded me a moment. It didn't set well with him that I'd go it alone. But he knew it was useless to argue. There was no reason in the world why he should be in the vehicle with me as I attempted to back it off the treacherous edge.

"Be careful, Bill," he said.

"She's never let me down yet."

He smiled. "Six-legged mountain goat, right?"

"Yep."

I inched my way back along the narrow, snow-covered portion of bridge until I reached the driver's door and climbed inside. Bundy followed, sidestepping cautiously past me until he was able to walk out in front of my vehicle. I turned the ignition key. The engine rumbled to life. I grabbed the steering wheel with both hands, took a deep breath, and eased the Bronco into reverse. There was a subtle clunk! as the transmission engaged. I released the emergency brake, my heart pounding in my chest. Then I pushed gently on the gas and felt the tires begin to move.

I didn't know what would happen next. I might just as easily slide right, and tumble into the frozen creek, as veer left to safety. But my tires held fast, biting into the snowpack like eagle's claws, they pulled my Bronco backwards, gradually drawing my dangling wheel up onto the bridge. With all four tires standing on firm surface, I looked at Bundy and gave him a jubilant thumbs up. He raised his arms and gestured for me to come straight ahead as he walked backwards along the frozen bridge. I put the Bronco into drive and began to inch forward.

"Good girl!" I murmured, as if my rugged chariot could hear. "I'm gonna treat you to some high-test, as soon as we get to town."

A bear cub lay dead before me, its black coat vivid against the blazing white snow. At a mere forty-five pounds, she was the smallest of three. The runt. Shot dead and left behind to be picked apart by coyotes and vultures. I could see where her two siblings had been killed. Their bodies carving a bloody furrow through the snow as they were dragged off. Human footprints indicating two perpetrators.

Deputy Zika had briefed me on the father and son he'd checked earlier, how their suspicious behavior caused him to backtrack them. There was no doubt they were responsible. Parents need to be role models for their children. How could a father raise his son this way? It saddened me to think of it.

I focused on the cub and began taking photographs. I knelt and examined it, methodically pushing my fingers through its thick fur to search for bullet holes. I found a single, dime-sized entrance hole, then turned the carcass over. The projectile went clean through, leaving no hope for ballistics; the trajectory of the wound clearly indicating she had been shot from below.

I stood and turned. A tall oak, surrounded by a carpet of trodden, red snow, illustrated what had happened here. As the frightened cubs clung to the tree for safety, they were systematically picked off, one by one, like cheap targets in some carnival shooting gallery.

Still, it wasn't illegal. And had the hunters-turned-poachers taken one bear each, they would have been legitimate kills. Not necessarily sportsmanlike, but legal just the same. The cubs were easy targets, fixed to the tree like magnets on a refrigerator, not scampering through the woods in a blur of motion. The hunters had all the time in the world to pick their targets. So why shoot all three? The answer came to me almost as soon as I asked myself the question. If they were huddled together, one above the next, a bullet coming from below could have penetrated all three cubs. I felt my temple begin to throb. If you're going to shoot cub bears out of a tree, the least you can do is take proper aim.

For a long time, it had been illegal to kill bear cubs in Pennsylvania. But two things changed that: First, a number of hunters were reluctant to turn in a cub they'd shot in mistake for an adult. For some, it was because they were embarrassed by their error, while others found it easier to leave the carcass in the woods. Why report it and have to pay a fifty-dollar fine plus lose the opportunity to kill a legal bear? Besides, who would know? As a result, bear cubs killed by mistake were being left in the woods to rot each year. It was inevitable—we knew that. What we didn't know, was how many. Fifty? One hundred? Five hundred? And the agency (rightfully) feared the unknown: That being what impact a high mortality rate in cub bears might have on the total population. How could we effectively manage the bear population if we didn't know how many were being killed by hunters each year?

Secondly, it's often impossible to tell the difference between a large cub bear and a small adult without examining their teeth (adult bears lose their smaller milk teeth and develop larger canines). This proved to be embarrassing, not just for the hunter but the officer as well, when someone brought a questionable bear into the Game Commission's Bear Check Station and we had to look in the critter's mouth to determine if it was an adult.

Sorry pal, this is a cub. We realize it looks like an adult because it weighs almost a hundred pounds. But it's just a big cub. So now we have to confiscate your bear in front of your buddies and make you pay a fine! Don't ya just love us?

Obviously, a hunter can't check a bear's teeth before pulling the trigger; so, we eventually came to our senses and made it legal to kill cub bears in Pennsylvania. But it's not encouraged by any means. We would hope that a cub bear would never be killed. Furthermore, examining a bear's choppers isn't the only way to separate cubs from adults. Adult bears are loners. Hunters who see bears traveling together during the November season can be certain they're seeing either a sow with her cubs or a group of cubs separated from their mother. It's time to make a choice: shoot or walk away.

I was certain that had been the scenario with the cubs killed here. The sow most likely shot earlier in the day, leaving the three orphaned cubs to wander through the woods until they were discovered by our suspects and killed while taking refuge in a tree.

Now the snowfall that had plagued me earlier in the day would come to my aid. The vast, white landscape becoming an open book, where boot prints, bear tracks, spent casings, and bits of hair and blood narrated the story for us, telling all we needed to know.

After photographing the crime scene, we began searching for physical evidence. Anything that might help prove the case in a court of law, if it went that far. I watched Deputy Zika crouch at the tree where the cubs were killed. He scooped up a handful of bloodstained snow. Something had caught his eye. A tiny piece of muscle tissue belonging to one of the cubs. Retrieving a small manila envelope from his coat pocket, he dropped the specimen inside for a DNA analysis.

Bundy was backtracking the three cubs through the snow. He came upon a splash of blood and a tuft of black fur. One of the cubs had been wounded there before reaching the tree. After photographing the evidence, he knelt and scraped everything into a small plastic bag and pocketed it.

The Crime Lab would be able to match the blood, muscle tissue, and fur we collected to the two missing cubs, as well as to any blood or hairs found on our suspect's pickup truck or hunting clothes. But it wouldn't tell us if the father and his son each shot one cub—making them legal kills—or if both cubs had been shot by the father alone, as we suspected. And what of the third cub?—the only one we could be certain was over the limit and unlawfully killed at this point. Would they claim it was dead when they got here? That someone else shot it and left it behind? Had it not been for the recent snow, the alibi might hold. But theirs were the only footprints we could find here. Fortunately, no other hunters had stumbled into the crime scene to track it up before we arrived. Hence, we were certain they were the poachers responsible, and as we started back to my patrol car with the illegal cub, I wondered what their story would be.

When we arrived, two bear cubs lay in the bed of a pickup truck parked in the driveway. I pulled behind the truck, purposely blocking it in, and stepped out to examine the carcasses. Both had been shot multiple times, the bullets traveling clean through. I glanced up at the house, a modest, wood-framed two-story situated on a quarter acre. Like most homes lining the village street, its exterior had been recently updated with vinyl siding. The surrounding landscape neat and trim. Not the typical poacher's lair by any means.

As I approached the front door, swirls of white smoke drifted from the chimney to disappear into a cobalt sky. The wind brisk on my face as I climbed three concrete steps and stood on the landing. I knocked. At my feet, a rubber doormat said, *Welcome.*

I doubted it.

The sound of plodding footsteps followed by the clack of a deadbolt being unlatched. I watched the brass doorknob turn. The door creaked open. I lifted my eyes and locked them upon a middle-aged woman wringing her hands, her face a map of apprehension.

"State Game Commission, Ma'am," I said. "I'm here concerning some bear cubs that were killed this morning."

"They've been expecting you, officer," she said. "Please. Come in out of the cold."

She turned, and I followed her down a short hall into a comfortable, wood-paneled den. The mounted heads of deer, bear, and various other critters adorned the walls. A man and a boy sat by a smoldering woodstove, their body language indicating they were ready to confess: arms resting heavily on their laps, fingers laced, chins on their chests like schoolboys at the principal's office.

"Guess you know why I'm here," I said.

The boy glanced at his father and turned away, his eyes to the floor.

"We know," said the elder. He lifted his chin and stared at me, lips pressed into a thin white line. "I've caused enough trouble for my family already. I've apologized to my wife and son. Now I'm apologizing to you, officer. I'm prepared to face the consequences; I just ask that you leave my boy out of this."

"If I can," I said. "What happened?"

He shrugged a heavy shoulder. "I overreacted. No doubt about it. We heard some shots back in the swamp. They sounded close. Next thing we know three bears are running toward us at full tilt. When I saw an opportunity for my son and me to fill our tags, I told him to shoot. He fired twice and missed, so I started shooting. I hit one of them but he kept on going and shinnied up a tree. The others hustled up after him. By the time we got there, they had climbed way up to the top. I knew I wounded one of them but couldn't tell which one it was. They all look the same, you know." He paused to glance at his son. The boy's eyes glued to the floor. "Anyway, they were all clustered together up there. I couldn't wait all day for them to come down, so I shot one out of the tree and told the boy to shoot one, too. He fired once . . . thought he missed. Fired again and both bears came down. It was a mistake. My fault. He did what I told him."

108

"Mistake kills are supposed to be reported immediately," I said. "That's not what happened here."

"My fault again, officer. It was my decision to leave the bear behind."

I looked at the boy. "Is that the way you remember it, son?"

He glanced up with frightened eyes. "Yes, sir," he said. "We didn't mean to kill three bears."

I didn't know why I bothered asking. The kid would've said anything his father told him to. He was scared half to death, and I didn't think it was me he was afraid of. I reckoned they had rehearsed their story long before I arrived, hoping I wouldn't fine the boy for his alleged mistake. And although I suspected that the father had killed all three cubs, it would be impossible to prove. The only thing I knew for sure, and could confirm in court, is that we had two hunters with three dead bears—one of which was over the limit.

Even if I believed their story, what happened wasn't a mistake; it was gross negligence. No chance of a fifty-dollar "mistake kill" fine here. Had they voluntarily turned in the third cub, a fine constituting full penalty would still have been in order. And because the Game Law provided that an individual could be prosecuted for causing another to violate the law, I arrested the father rather than his son for the unlawful killing of the third cub. The penalty in those days was eight hundred dollars, for which he later pled guilty and paid in full. Additionally, he was slapped with three years revocation of his hunting and trapping privileges.

Unfortunately, I didn't think the penalty would have much of an affect on the man, other than to make him more wary the next time around. Job security, I supposed. My primary concern was for his son. I could only hope that his run-in with the law would leave a lasting impression, and that if we ever met again, it would be on much better terms.

Everything must be like something, so what is this like?
                                                    ~ E.M. Forster

Head Games

CLYDE COOTER SAW THE DEER FIRST, even though he was driving at a pretty good clip while watching the road so he wouldn't run into anything.

"There's one!" he cried, bringing his pickup truck to a grinding stop. His son, Cletus, and Billy Bob Bodean were both sitting next to him. They swung their heads and stared into the autumn woods. Fifty yards away, an eight-point buck stood broadside to them. Still as a statue, the deer watched their truck as it came to rest along the road's edge.

"Quick! Hand me the gun," said Clyde. He reached past his son and took the thirty-thirty rifle from Billy Bob who'd been holding it. Pointing the barrel out his open window, Clyde eased the stock against his boney shoulder and took aim.

But as he was about to pull the trigger, Cletus tapped him gently on the back.

Clyde snapped his head around, clearly agitated. "What do you want, boy? I'm trying to shoot!"

"Pop, that's Faylene Ford's house right there. She's gonna be mighty sore if you shoot a deer in her front yard."

Clyde slid his eyes to the right. A short distance away her driveway arced into the woods before disappearing behind the house. He didn't see a car parked, and nobody was watching from the big picture window out front. It looked like a safe shot (*safe* to Clyde meant he probably wouldn't get caught). He brought the rifle back to his shoulder and squinted into the scope. Then he leveled the crosshairs at the sweet spot behind the deer's front shoulder. He touched the trigger with his index finger, exhaled slowly, and squeezed.

BOOM!

The deer tucked its tail and kicked back like a bucking bronco as the fatal gunshot echoed off the surrounding hills. Then it bolted straight toward Faylene Ford's house as if it hadn't been hit at all, but was just scared. When the deer reached Faylene's back yard, a distance of only eighty feet, it dropped dead. Struck through the center of both lungs, the bullet had severed the large blood vessels at the top of the heart as it bored through its rib cage.

Clyde was not surprised to see the deer fall. Born and raised right there in Muskrat Hollow, he'd become a legendary hunter to the local residents. They even referred to him as Deerslayer after the famed woodsman from James Fenimore Cooper's *Leatherstocking Tales*.

Clyde handed Billy Bob the rifle and started driving down Faylene's driveway after his prize. When he pulled up to the carcass, only yards from the patio door, they were all surprised to see that several bushels of apples and corn had been scattered in the yard.

"No wonder the deer's so stout," said Billy Bob. "Faylene's been feeding it fresh produce!"

The three men leaped from the truck and circled the heavy eight-pointer. "Nice of her to fatten up the herd for us," said Clyde. "Should make for some fine steaks and burgers."

"Mouth is watering like a rabid 'coon already," said Billy Bob, the mental image setting off a barrage of raucous laughter between the two men. But their hilarity was cut abruptly short when they saw that Cletus wasn't laughing along with them. Instead, he stood woodenly and stared right past them. Both men frowned as they realized their backs were turned to Faylene's house while Cletus faced it. And he was wide-eyed as a hoot owl in a lightening storm.

Clyde and Billy Bob recognized at once that they'd miscalculated. Why, they could feel Faylene's eyes boring into them even before they turned.

She stood glowering at them through the glass door, arms folded tightly across her frail chest. Her hair fell past her shoulders, just like it did as a teenager. But she was sixty now, the hair frizzled and wild. A small woman, standing five-feet-two and barely more than a hundred pounds soaking wet, her leathery face was lined with wrinkles from too much sun and too many cigarettes. But her hazel eyes were clear and cold as a mountain brook, and the men became petrified by her glacial stare.

The blast from Clyde's rifle had brought her out of a deep slumber. She worked nights waitressing at the diner down town, and had only gone to bed an hour ago when the gunshot jolted her awake. Leaping from her bed, she dashed to the bedroom window and saw an old Chevrolet pickup coming toward her house. Three men inside. She recognized the truck immediately.

Lord have mercy! Don't tell me they shot one of my deer.

Faylene ran from the bedroom into the living room, hair flying wildly about her head. She peered out the big glass door that opened to her back yard. She saw the eight-point buck lying dead in the grass. It sickened her. She turned and stormed to the kitchen phone. Stabbing the buttons with an index finger, she called nine-one-one. County Emergency Management answered, said they'd connect her immediately to the appropriate agency. Waiting, she fumbled through a drawer for her cigarettes. With trembling hands, she tapped out a Salem from the pack and lit one. She could hear the truck come to a stop outside. Then came the sound of boisterous laughter. Cavemen! Ruthless slobs! Oh, how she hated them. She took a long pull on her cigarette. Thought about the revolver hidden in her bedroom. A single woman. Alone. Frightened. Three armed men outside. It would be self-defense—

"Game Commission . . ."

"Who?" she said into the phone. Her mind still focused on the gun.

"Pennsylvania Game Commission, ma'am. Can I help you?"

She blurted her address and explained what had happened there. *"The men are here now!"* she had cried. *"Please, hurry!"*

Slamming down the phone, she crushed her cigarette in the kitchen sink, her fear suddenly transforming into a cold and terrible fury. The audacity of these impudent, shameless louts! Whose property *was* this anyway? She turned on her heels (she was barefooted) and marched to the glass door to confront them.

That's when Clyde and Billy Bob stopped heehawing and wheeled around after seeing Cletus's eyeballs had grown big as saucers.

She slid open the heavy glass door and stepped out to face them, hands on her hips. "Whose scatterbrained idea was it to shoot that poor harmless creature?" she hissed.

Clyde and Billy Bob looked at each other and swallowed hard.

Clyde said, "Ma'am, I . . . I . . ."

"You what?" she snapped.

He opened his mouth again but nothing came out except a thin croaking sound.

She turned to Cletus. "What about you? Cat got your tongue, too?"

Cletus didn't offer a word. He just stood there slack-jawed and quiet as a milk snake in a hay bale.

"Well?" said Faylene. "Mean to say there ain't one of you man enough to speak up?"

Billy Bob was grimacing like his hemorrhoids were on fire. He raised both hands, fingers splayed in a gesture of submission. "We done wrong. I know. I know. And you got every right to be mad, Fay. But—"

"Don't you call me Fay!" she snapped. "Only my friends can call me that. And you ain't no friend of mine, Billy Bob Bodean!"

Billy Bob's face dropped into an enormous frown, taking on the appearance of a child who just had his favorite toy taken away. Fay had always been Fay when he stopped by the diner in town. She'd have a pleasant smile for him when he sat at the front counter (like he always would) and ordered his food, too. And he knew that she knew that he sat at the counter so he could be close to her. It was no secret that Billy Bob liked the food at the diner only half as much as he liked watching Fay work.

So, in pathetic self-defense, he blurted, "It was Clyde!" (He couldn't help himself. His heart was broken.) "Clyde saw the deer. Clyde shot the deer. It was all his doing, Fay— I mean, Faylene."

She leveled her icy gaze on Clyde. "You are a despicable man, Clyde Cooter. I've been feeding this deer all year long, and now you've gone and shot it dead right on my lawn!

You got no right to do that. No right at all! I want all of you off my property right now!"

Clyde looked at the buck for a moment and suddenly found his voice. "What are you going to do with the deer?"

Her eyes narrowed into slits. "What did you say?"

"I just wondered if we could keep it, that's all. Or do you want to eat it?"

Faylene shook her head in disgust. "Don't you dare touch that poor critter, Clyde Cooter. Now, I'm going back inside to get my revolver. And if any of you are still here when I come back, I'll shoot you in both kneecaps!"

F aylene Ford stood over the deer as I drove up her narrow driveway. She was dressed in blue jeans and a gray Penn State sweatshirt, a cigarette in one hand and a coffee cup in the other.

I parked close by and stepped out to meet her. The corn and apples scattered about told me she'd been feeding the deer and probably considered them her pets. I expected her to be upset and hoped she wasn't a flake.

"State Game Commission, Ma'am," I said.

She nodded.

"Do you know who shot the deer?"

"Know him!" she scoffed. "Grew up with him! He lives down the road a piece. Name's Clyde Cooter. His son, Cletus, and Billy Bob Bodean were both with him."

"I know who they are."

"Suspected so. I wish you'd go and arrest them or something. I mean, seriously, they can't go around shooting deer in peoples' yards like this. They've been doing it for years, and the law's never caught up with him yet."

"I expect that'll change today," I said.

She turned her face and stared down the driveway. Then she took a drag of her cigarette and nodded stiffly. A plume of blue-gray smoke streamed from her nostrils. "They shot it from the road, too," she said. Then she turned toward me, her eyes moist and searching. "I'll never understand those people. What gives them the right to go around slaughtering God's creatures like that? Why, I hear Clyde Cooter has twenty-five deer hanging in his barn right now."

The news gave me a jolt. Although I thought it was an exaggerated number, the fact that the rumor was floating around at all meant that Cooter likely had some illegal deer in his barn. I intended to find out just how many.

"I'll be heading over to the Cooter farm as soon as I leave here, ma'am. You can rest assured that he'll be paying for this deer, as well as any others he's killed unlawfully."

Faylene nodded solemnly, a teardrop tracking down her weathered cheek. "You got a reputation around here, in case you don't know it. I want to thank you for getting here so promptly, too. Helps put my mind at ease."

I nodded an acknowledgement. "I'll be taking the deer for evidence after I snap a few pictures. I also want to look around a bit, see if I can find where it was standing when they shot it."

She crushed her cigarette under the toe of a Reebok sneaker. "Help yourself. I'm going inside to watch TV. Read a book. Anything to make me forget what happened here today."

"Yes, ma'am," I said.

The Cooters lived in a singlewide trailer. The lane leading up to it was dirt. Three wooden doghouses sat adjacent to each other like sentry boxes at the top of the drive. But none contained dogs, for three surly mongrels circled my patrol car, barking at my tires as I rolled up the dusty lane and parked adjacent to the trailer.

I popped open my glove box, grabbed a big handful of Milk-Bones, and hurled them out the window over the hood of my patrol car. Two dogs scampered after the treats. The third, a particularly ugly black and gray wolfish-looking thing, stood below my window and stared at me guardedly. The hair on its neck bristled. "Good boy!" I said, dropping a biscuit at its feet. He never looked down. Instead, a low, menacing growl came from the back of his throat—

"Brutus! No!" came a shout from the trailer.

I looked up. An elderly woman stood at the front door, holding it open. "He won't hurt you," she hollered.

I'd heard that tune before.

Ambushed by three different dogs earlier in my career (and bitten twice), I instantly recalled an incident where I'd mistakenly went to the wrong house on a nuisance wildlife complaint. I noticed a "BEWARE OF DOG!" sign posted at the door but didn't see evidence of a hound lurking anywhere. I knew that some people who didn't own dogs would post these signs to deter thieves and salesmen, and suspected that was the case. Knocking on the glass front door, I could see straight through the house to a large picture window that opened to the back yard. A woman was hanging laundry. I circled the house to meet her. *Hello*, I called as I stepped around the corner. She turned. A white bed sheet in her hand. Face frozen in astonishment. *Don't move!* she warned. Then, *Lobo! Lobo come!* My chest tightened. Why Lobo? Why couldn't it be Pooky or Fifi? Suddenly, breaking from the tall fields behind her house, a large German shepherd appeared. At first, he didn't see me. The woman reached for his collar as he padded up to her. She almost had him. But at the last second, he turned his head. He froze instantly. Astonished, like his master, by my presence. Then he charged. (*BEWARE OF DOG!*) He was on me in seconds. I couldn't risk taking a shot at him. The woman stood directly in my line of fire. With no time to think, I did a quick snap-kick, my booted right foot smashing into his tender snout. He stepped back. An arm's length away, I reached for my revolver, fully expecting a second attack. Instead, the dog shook his head and expelled a kind of woofing sneeze, then he turned and loped back to the woman. I never forgot how close I'd come to being chewed up that day.

I returned my thoughts to the woman in the trailer. "I'd appreciate it if you'd put your dog on a leash, ma'am."

She stepped cautiously down three rickety wooden steps to a small patch of lawn. "Brutus!" she cried. "Get into your house right now!"

Brutus lowered his ears and looked at her for a moment. Then he snapped his head back toward me and licked his chops nervously.

"Brutus!" the woman called. "You heard me." She clapped her hands and pointed to a doghouse. "Go on!"

The wolfish mongrel looked at her again, as if giving the old woman one last chance to change her mind. She put her hands on her hips and hissed at him sharply. "Brutus!"

With that, he let out a long, pitiful whine and trotted off to lie at the entrance of his doghouse.

The woman turned to me and smiled. She was in her late sixties with a soft, pleasant face and snow-white hair combed into a tight bun. "Really. He won't hurt you."

I opened my door, slid off the seat, and stood with my door hanging open in case Brutus got up and came after me. He had his big head on his paws, his feral, yellow eyes studying me critically.

"State Game Commission, ma'am. I'm here to see Clyde Cooter."

Behind her, the front door opened suddenly, and a man who looked to be in his twenties, started to walk out. He saw me and quickly ducked back inside.

She glanced over her shoulder at the door as it slammed shut. She frowned. "That was my son, Cletus. You must be looking for him, too."

"Yes, ma'am. He was involved in a Game Law violation this morning along with Clyde and Billy Bob Bodean."

Her brow fell as she digested the news. "I'm Mrs. Cooter," she said. "We sure don't need trouble with the law. Clyde isn't here but you might as well come inside. Don't you worry about ol' Brutus, either. He'll stay put as long as I tell him to."

She turned and started toward the trailer. I followed. The two mongrels that had run off before came scampering from underneath my Ford Expedition. Both dogs circled me, wagging their tails and barking excitedly as I walked across the front lawn. I reached into my coat pocket and tossed each one a biscuit as I trailed the old woman into her home.

Gertie Mae Cooter walked to her cupboard and took a white, ceramic cup from a shelf. "Coffee?" she asked. "I was about to have some myself."

"Yes, thank you," I said. Normally I would have refused. But I could hear the apprehension in her voice and thought a shared cup might bring her less worry. She spooned some Maxwell House into two empty cups and took a simmering kettle from the gas stove. "Cream and sugar is on the table."

"Black's fine," I answered.

"Well . . ." she said, turning and nodding toward the kitchen table, "aren't you going to sit down?"

I pulled a chair and sat. Gertie Mae set a steaming cup in front of me and poured another for herself. Resting the kettle on the stove, she lowered the flame and took a chair directly across from me. "Hope you don't mind instant," she said, stirring her cup.

"Drink it all the time." In truth, I almost never did.

She smiled warily at me.

Cletus sat on a couch in an adjacent room ten feet away. He was watching cartoons with a boy who looked about six or seven. Although the room was open to the kitchen, he pretended not to notice me. Gertie Mae watched him with a raised brow. "Cletus, you're being rude," she called. Come in here and sit down."

Cletus sunk his head into his shoulders and stared at her with painful eyes.

"Don't act as if we're invisible, young man. You know right well this officer isn't here to talk to me!"

He clucked his tongue and pushed himself reluctantly off the couch, his jaw bunched tight. "Stay here, Codie," he told the boy.

Cletus Cooter was six feet tall and skinny as a rail. His hair was like dried hay, teeth broken and decayed. He took a chair next to his mother, rested his scrawny arms on the table, and laced his soiled fingers together.

"Morning, Cletus," I said.

He nodded sullenly.

I glanced toward the child in the other room. He sat on the couch with his hands behind his head, giggling at Wile E. Coyote hanging in midair and blinking stupidly before plunging ten thousand feet into a desert canyon. *Poof!*

Road Runner smiled at Codie and said, *"Meep, Meep!"*

Codie giggled with delight.

"Cute kid," I said.

Cletus nodded. "Takes after his mom."

I took a sip of my coffee. "Know why I'm here?"

"Yup. Faylene Ford," said Cletus. "She's mighty upset."

"I don't blame her."

Cletus studied me. I could almost hear the wheels in his skull turning as he tried to come up with an explanation. After a minute he asked, "What's the law on shooting deer for crop damage?"

"If you farm for a living, you can shoot deer for crop damage," I said flatly.

Cletus smiled. "Year round?"

I glanced at his mother. Her lips were parted; a look of uncertainty crossed her face as she stared at her son.

"It's December, Cletus," I said. "You don't have any crops growing right now, do you?"

His smile slowly evaporated. "No . . . I guess we don't."

"Besides, the deer have to be on your property," I said, "not the neighbor's down the road."

"But deer wander about. They don't stay just on our land."

"I understand, Cletus. But the law is the law. You can only shoot deer on property that you farm. And you have to report each deer to us within twenty-four hours, remove the entrails, and keep the carcass in a safe location so we can pick it up."

Cletus hesitated. He glanced at his mother and back to me. "Then Faylene's deer don't count?"

"Afraid not."

Gertie Mae said, "Cletus, did you shoot a deer on Faylene Ford's property?"

"No, ma'am."

"Well, who did?"

"I told him not to, but he wouldn't listen."

"Who wouldn't listen?"

"Dad," muttered Cletus. "Billy Bob and me was with him, but we didn't do nothing."

Gertie May looked at me and rolled her eyes. "Clyde can't help himself sometimes," she said apologetically. "He loves his deer hunting too much."

"I hear they call him Deerslayer," I said.

She shook her head. "Don't know why. He only kills what we can eat. But rumors fly. One came back to me recently that we're supposed to have twenty-five deer in our barn. That's just plain crazy!"

"I heard the same rumor, ma'am."

She snorted. "You're welcome to look in the barn if you want. We got nothing to hide."

Cletus whipped his head at her. "Ma . . . !"

"Now you hush, son. I want this man to go ahead and look for himself, so folks around here will finally know the truth."

"But he don't even have a search warrant, Ma!"

"Never mind that, son. I said he can look."

By the way Cletus was acting, I suspected there was something in the barn he didn't want me to see. Perhaps the rumor about twenty-five deer was true after all.

Cletus said, "Barn's locked. Dad has the only key."

"When will your father be back?" I asked him.

Cletus shrugged. Gertie Mae answered. "Any time now," she said. "He hasn't had his breakfast yet."

I stood from the table and pushed in my chair. "I'd like to take a walk over to the barn. Just to look around. I want you to come too, Cletus. Keep the dogs off my heels."

"You got that right," he scoffed. "No way you're gonna be snooping around here by yourself."

Little Codie Cooter skipped along behind us as we walked out to the barn. Brutus was sleeping soundly, the warm afternoon sun reflecting off his soft coat as he lay in front of his doghouse. The other two mongrels started to follow but Cletus turned on them. He stooped and picked up a handful of stones, hurling them one by one at the dogs. He threw fast and hard, like a Major League pitcher. *Thwack! Thwack!* Both dogs yelped in pain as the granite missiles struck their tender rumps. I watched them scurry back under my patrol car for shelter.

Cletus opened his hand and let the remaining stones fall to the ground. "Don't know why they're under your car," he wondered out loud. "They usually shy away from strangers."

"He gives them cookies Daddy!" said Codie. "I saw him. He's a nice man!"

Cletus looked askance at me and shrugged. "Up to him if he wants to waste good money."

Codie scratched his head and looked back at the dogs. Then he picked up a stone and hurled it at them for good measure. "And stay there!" he shouted.

I reproved him with a stern look. *Like father, like son!*

As we continued single file across the brown stubbed remains of a cornfield, I saw a white metal-sided pole barn fifty yards ahead. The size of a three-car garage, it had an overhead door wide enough for large farm vehicles and a single exterior side-entry door fortified with a deadbolt. The overhead looked like a roll-up that could only be opened from inside the barn.

"I got no key," Cletus reminded me as I followed him alongside the windowless building. "We can't get in. I don't know why you're wasting your time."

While making our way to the side door, I noticed a cavity in the ground at the bottom edge of the building. It looked like a dog had once dug its way into the barn, and the hole never backfilled. As we passed, I watched Codie from the corner of my eye. He dropped to his belly and squirmed into the opening, his little legs disappearing up inside the barn.

Cletus grabbed the doorknob and jiggled it hard. "Locked!" he called over his shoulder. "Just like I told you." He turned suddenly, his eyes searching left and right. "Hey! Where'd Codie go?"

"I'm in here, Dad!" cried his son from opposite the door. "I can open it from inside!"

Cletus's chest deflated like a toy balloon. "What the . . . !"

Poor Codie had thought his father wanted to get into the barn all along and wanted to surprise him by showing how resourceful he could be.

Cletus shook his head with grim resignation. "Forgot all about that danged hole!" he muttered.

Inside the barn, I saw not twenty-five deer but a single carcass. Gutted, skinned, and decapitated, it lay on a wooden table at the far end of the earthen floor directly across from us. There was little else. An old Ford tractor squatted to my left; a collection of assorted junk and rusted farm equipment scattered here and there. Otherwise, the barn was conspicuously empty.

I moved toward the deer. Cletus followed, trailed by his son. The carcass looked fresh, perhaps a few hours old. The animal had been shot once, just behind the front shoulder. "Where's the head?" I asked.

Cletus's Adam's apple danced like a yo-yo on a string as he gazed at the raw carcass. "Don't ask me!" he moaned. "It ain't *my* deer."

I looked questioningly at the boy. He turned his palms up and shrugged.

I said to Cletus, "With no head and being gutted like this, it's impossible to tell whether the deer is a buck or a doe . . ."

Cletus continued to stare at the carcass.

" . . . Which makes this an illegal deer."

"What?" he yelped. "Just 'cause it don't have no head?"

"That's right. Unless you can find it for me."

He pushed his lips into pouting frown. "I don't know nothing about it. I never even saw it before. This is my *dad's* barn. You gotta ask *him* if you want to know anything more."

Just then, the laboring chug of an approaching engine began to filter into the barn. A vehicle was coming our way. I strode to the door and peeked outside. A green Chevy pickup had turned into the farm and started up the driveway toward the house.

Cletus shuffled alongside me to look for himself.

"That your dad?" I asked.

"Yup. That's him," said Cletus.

When Clyde saw my patrol car parked by his house, he knew it meant trouble. He could've just kept on driving, too. But that would only have put off the inevitable. Clyde wasn't stupid. Impulsive and uneducated, perhaps, but not stupid.

Besides, like Gertie Mae had said, he hadn't had breakfast yet.

Clyde was sitting at the kitchen table sipping his coffee and watching Gertie May scramble eggs when we walked into the trailer. He looked up at me and nodded at a chair opposite him. "Morning, warden," he said. "Have a seat."

Cletus and Codie shuffled into the next room to plunk down on the couch and turn on cartoons. Bugs Bunny's sassy voice came blaring into the kitchen: *"Eh . . . What's up doc?"* followed by Yosemite Sam's hostile, throaty bawl: *"Okay varmint, say your prayers!"*—

"Turn that down!" hollered Gertie Mae.

"Yes, ma'am," said Cletus. He grabbed awkwardly for the remote and squelched the volume to an agreeable murmur.

Gertie Mae rolled her eyes at me. "Cletus loves his cartoons."

I smiled and nodded as if I understood.

Coffee, warden?" she asked.

"No. But thank you, ma'am."

I pulled a chair from the table. The last cup had been so strong it seemed to roll down my throat directly into my bladder. Any more and I would've been squirming in my seat.

"Had your breakfast?" asked Clyde. "Got plenty of eggs."

"Thanks," I said. "I've already eaten."

If there was one thing I hated, it was having to arrest folks who were . . . well, likable. There just wasn't any other way to describe them. It was obvious they had very little money, and I was certain any deer they killed would provide food for the entire family. That they were outlaws, I had no doubt. But these weren't trophy poachers who skull-capped deer for their antlers and left the carcasses for scavengers to eat. They were basically, nice people.

Clyde said, "I guess you want to talk to me about Faylene's deer."

"Yes."

"I shot it," he replied flatly. "Guess she likened it to some kind of pet or something. She's pretty upset, too. But it was a legal buck."

"Not really," I said. "For one thing, it was a safety zone violation."

Clyde looked confused. "I didn't see any posters saying her property was a safety zone! It's deer season. I saw an eight-point buck and shot it . . . legally, I thought."

125

"She doesn't have to post her property," I told him. "State law says you have to be at least one hundred and fifty yards from someone's house or barn when you're hunting. That includes whatever you're shooting at. The deer you killed was less than thirty yards from Faylene's house."

Clyde nodded slowly as he digested the news. "Then I was wrong."

"You also shot the deer from the road," I added. "That's road hunting. And it's also illegal."

Gertie Mae put a plate of scrambled eggs and some bacon along with two slices of buttered toast in front of Clyde. He looked up at her with worried eyes; then he touched her hand with his fingertips and smiled softly. "Thank you, Mae."

Blinking back tears, she turned away. Then she went to the sink and began washing dishes.

Clyde stabbed at his plate with his fork and shoveled a gob of eggs into his mouth.

I let him eat.

He polished off the eggs and bacon and washed them down with a long drink of coffee. Then he said, "Okay. What's the fine? I know there's gotta be a fine or you wouldn't be here."

"That depends," I said.

Clyde picked up a slice of toast, broke it in half, and looked at me. "Depends?" he said. "On what?"

"On how honestly you answer my questions."

"What do you want to know?"

"Who killed the deer in your barn?"

Clyde examined his toast for a moment. He shook his head. "I don't want to get anybody in trouble."

"You're saying you didn't kill it, then?"

"That's right."

"Well, who did?"

He frowned and looked away.

"Do you know where the head is?"

"No."

"Well then, somebody already *is* in trouble. Want it to be you?"

"No, sir."

"Look, Clyde, the deer is in your barn. It's a fresh kill. And it's a game law violation if you can't produce the head. It'll be your fine to pay if you don't start talking. Now I'll ask you again . . . last chance . . . who killed the deer?"

Clyde nodded in submission. "I can't afford to pay for one illegal deer let alone two. Billy Bob Bodean killed the one in the barn. He thought it was a legal six-pointer when he shot it, but when he walked up to it he saw it was only a four-point buck. He asked me to keep it in my barn so nobody would see it."

"That makes you an accomplice," I said. "It also makes you liable for the same five hundred dollar fine as Mr. Bodean."

Clyde glanced helplessly at Gertie Mae. She turned from the sink with a dishtowel clenched in her hands, eyes wide with alarm.

Seeing this, I said, "Look, Clyde, Mrs. Cooter, I asked you to be honest with me and you were. I'm not going to prosecute you for the deer in the barn. But I want you to understand what can happen when you do something like this."

"I appreciate that, warden," said Clyde.

I leaned forward to emphasize a point: "But if it ever happens again, I guarantee you I won't overlook it. Understand?"

Gertie Mae and Clyde shook their heads simultaneously. Gertie Mae said, "It won't *ever* happen again, officer. I promise you."

"I'm not letting you off scot-free, either," I continued. "Clyde, your deer was shot from the road and killed in a safety zone. We're talking about close to a thousand dollars in fines . . ."

He winced with gritted teeth.

" . . . but like I said, you've been honest with me, so I'm not going to prosecute you for every violation. Just one. The safety zone. We're talking more like two hundred."

Clyde closed his eyes and blew a sigh of relief.

"Now," I said, "how about directions to Billy Bob's house. . ."

Come in!" boomed a deep and stony voice. The tone more like a command than an invitation.

I opened the door and stepped into Billy Bob Bodean's darkened living room. The TV was on. Cops and robbers. Bodean peered at me critically from an oversized recliner, then he pointed his remote at the set and switched it off.

"State Game Commission," I said. "I'm here about the deer you killed—the one in Mr. Cooter's barn."

"What about it?" he grunted. He stood and walked toward me. "How'd you find out about it anyway?"

Billy Bob Bodean was an intimidating figure. A giant, in fact. He looked like a professional wrestler with his heavy arms and barrel chest. A broad, protruding forehead made his beady eyes set way back into his skull. The flesh on his brow thick and meaty and lined with deep wrinkles. He had a ruddy complexion and a bulbous nose that was crooked from an old break. He wore his orange-red hair in a comb-over from left to right to cover his balding head. And he had a thick, flowing beard the same odd color as his hair.

"It's a short-horned spike," he said. "And I got a doe license to make it legal."

"We must not be talking about the same deer," I said mockingly. "This is the one that's skinned and headless—the one you thought was a six-point buck until you walked up to the carcass."

Billy Bob's face turned livid. "Where'd you hear that story?"

"Clyde Cooter."

"Cooter!" he scoffed. "That no good weasel! Did he also tell you about the deer he shot at Faylene Ford's?"

"He already filled me in."

The news seemed to stun Billy Bob. He'd obviously wanted to get even with Clyde for ratting him out. He pulled on his beard and blinked at me in slow deliberation. "Clyde told you about it?"

"That's right," I said. "He answered me honestly when I confronted him. I admire him for that."

"Well, ain't that sweet," sneered Billy Bob. "You can admire him all you want; but I'm here to tell you I ain't done nothing wrong, so I got nothing to confess."

Billy Bob looked like he wanted to pick me up and body-slam me into oblivion. I steeled myself and pushed on with my questions. "Why would Clyde tell me you shot an illegal four-point buck if you didn't? Are you two enemies? Does he have some reason to bring trouble your way?"

"I don't care what Clyde Cooter told you!" he insisted. His voice grew louder, more impatient. "It was a legal deer, and I got a doe license for it. Want to see it?"

"What I want to see is the deer's head," I told him. "Then we can take a look at your hunting license."

"I don't have the head."

"Where is it?"

Billy Bob shrugged dismissively. "I threw it in the river."

I could see that he wasn't going to admit anything. I suspected the head was buried in his back yard someplace or stuffed in a trashcan. Whatever. It really didn't matter. I'd given him an opportunity to produce it and he refused. That was all I needed to prosecute him for poaching. Evidently, Bodean thought he had me over a barrel: If I couldn't find the head, I couldn't prove his deer was illegal. And he was right. I could not. Which is precisely why the Pennsylvania Game and Wildlife Code states that unless the head of a deer is attached in a natural manner and properly tagged, the possession, transportation or control of said carcass becomes prima facie evidence of an unlawful kill, and that the head must be produced immediately upon demand of an officer.

I didn't bother to tell him about that. Instead, I let him continue to gloat, thinking he had me.

"The deer is illegal," I said. "I'll be filing citations against you soon. You can tell your story to a judge, see how he feels." I turned to walk out the door.

"Then I'll see you in court," he promised. "And after I win at the trial, I'm gonna sue you for violating my rights!"

Trials are often complicated. I couldn't simply appear in court, show the judge a copy of the law, and then expect him to find Billy Bob Bodean guilty of poaching. Judges don't always rule on the black and white of a case; they like to probe into the gray area before making a decision. And the fact that Bodean's game law violation mandated a five hundred dollar fine plus the loss of his hunting and trapping privileges, might cause a judge to extend a gracious benefit of doubt to the defendant.

That's why I found myself back at Clyde Cooter's place later that morning. I asked if he'd be willing to testify against Billy Bob Bodean in court. He was reluctant. I didn't blame him.

"Look," I said, "I've done this sort of thing before. I'll have the judge subpoena you to court, which means you're lawfully compelled to be there. When I call on you to testify, the first thing I'll ask is if you received a court order to appear before the judge. You'll answer yes, and Bodean will see that you had no choice but to show up. He might even cancel his request for a hearing and plead guilty once he learns that you've been subpoenaed."

"But how's he gonna find out?" Clyde asked innocently.

"You've associated with Bodean for a long time, right?"

"Yes."

"Tell him. Tell him not to expect you to lie for him in court, too."

Clyde drummed his fingers on the kitchen table and considered what I'd told him. He looked at Gertie Mae. She nodded.

"Guess I got no choice, once I get the subpoena," he said. "Besides, you've been plenty fair with me. I owe you that much."

Three months passed. The trial lasted just under one hour. Billy Bob Bodean was determined to have his day in court. And by the look the judge gave him when he strode into the room, Bodean was no stranger to the system.

I called my star eyewitness to the stand, and the judge swore him in.

"Did you receive a subpoena ordering you to appear in court today?" I asked Clyde.

"Yes," he answered.

From here, I took him back to the day I came to his house and discovered Bodean's deer inside the pole barn. Clyde testified that he'd been hunting with Billy Bob Bodean when Bodean shot the four-point buck. He stated that Bodean realized the deer was illegal when he walked up to it and that that was why he disposed of the head and then asked Clyde if he could hide the carcass in his barn.

Even with Clyde's incriminating testimony, Bodean still wanted to take the stand to defend himself. He claimed that Clyde was lying through his teeth—that he'd been hoodwinked by the game warden into falsely testifying against him in exchange for charges being dropped on the deer he killed on Faylene Ford's property. He insisted that his deer was a legal short-horned buck and waved a hunting license in the judge's face while proclaiming his innocence.

But I had anticipated his defense. Hence, I didn't prosecute him for killing an unlawful deer. The citation was for failure to produce the head of a big game animal upon demand of an officer. Plain and simple. The only time in my thirty-two years as a conservation officer that I'd ever arrested anyone under that particular charge. And when the judge considered Clyde Cooter's testimony, and then took into account Bodean's incredulous declarations, it was a no-brainer for him.

Billy Bob Bodean decided not to appeal the judge's decision and paid his fine in full. Six months later, he received a letter from the Game Commission telling him that his hunting and trapping privileges were revoked for three years.

He continued to poach deer over the next decade, and I had several more run-ins with him until I retired from service.

Clyde and Cletus Cooter managed to behave themselves ever since. I never had a problem with them after that day.

Train up a child in the way he should go; and when he is old, he will not depart from it.

~ The Holy Bible

Fallout

SKINNY LENNY CHUNK was a career poacher. Each deer season my phone would ring off the hook with complaints about his unlawful road hunting. It didn't matter whose property he trespassed on, either. Any deer within gun range of a highway was a deer worth taking.

I remember the day he shot a doe that was standing in his neighbor's front yard. Lenny stopped his pickup truck in the middle of the road, pointed a rifle out the window, shot it dead. Then he proceeded to gut the carcass where it fell, less than twenty feet from the man's porch.

Lenny's neighbor called me to register a complaint. But when I asked if he would testify against him in court, he adamantly refused, stating that he feared Lenny would torch his house. When I said I'd been hearing that excuse for over twenty years but never had a poacher retaliate against a witness by setting their house on fire—it would be aggravated felony arson punishable by ten years in prison, he replied by saying, "You don't know Skinny Lenny. He doesn't think; he simply reacts. Don't ever turn your back on him."

He was right. I didn't know him. That was primarily because everyone who complained to me about Lenny Chunk was afraid to confront him. They would tell me what he'd done and then ask me to leave them out of it, hoping I'd catch him red-handed some day. But my district covered a lot of territory, and I couldn't spend all my time in Lenny Chunk's back yard waiting for him to break the law.

It was frustrating to know that a hardened poacher operated with impunity in my district and that I was unable to catch him.

I'll never forget the year I got calls about his road hunting every day for the entire doe season. But all I ever heard from the complainants was, *I don't want to get involved!* or *I'm afraid of retaliation!* or *I could get burned out!*

That is, until I received a phone call from a woman who caught Lenny Chunk road hunting with another man and a teenage boy and was willing to testify about it in court . . .

Orville Odenbock was the only person in the world who could address Lenny by his nickname, Skinny, and not get punched in the nose. Lenny had been tagged with the moniker back in grade school and always hated it. Although he was a lean and undernourished child, he was also calloused from daily farm chores and would promptly beat down any kid who dared call him that name.

Now, Orville was dying of cancer. But he could still get around pretty well. For that reason, Lenny wanted him to have first crack at a deer when they found one. After all, the two men had been pals for years, and this might be Orville's last season. Problem was, they'd been driving all over creation for the past two hours and hadn't seen a single tail.

Then: "Look there!" gushed Lenny. "Must be fifteen or twenty of them! You can take your pick, Orvy."

Orville pumped the brake and brought his pickup truck to an easy stop. They had come upon a two-story house surrounded by several acres of low grass on their right. Alongside the house, a band of deer grazed peacefully under a cold, gray sky.

Lenny's twelve-year-old son, Sammy, was sitting between the two men holding a lever-action Marlin between his knees, preparing to heft it to Orville.

Because the deer were on the opposite side of the road, Orville had to risk spooking the herd by exiting the vehicle in order to make the shot.

He cracked open his door and reached for the gun without looking back. Sammy obediently passed it to him. Orville felt the smooth wooden stock of the rifle, grasped hold of it and swung the muzzle forward, never taking his eyes off the deer as he slipped outside and slid his body along the front fender.

Orville leaned over the hood, propped his elbows on the warm metal surface for support, and steadied his rifle for a clean shot. Because he did all his hunting from a vehicle, a scope wasn't necessary. Open sights, at close range, worked just fine.

It looked like a seventy-yard shot. Challenging, perhaps, but doable, he thought. He squinted into the iron sights and leveled them on a fat doe. Then he slowly squeezed the trigger.

Click!

What the . . . !

He checked the safety.

Danged Sammy! The kid left it on! Why did Lenny have to bring him along?

Orville pushed off the safety and thumbed the hammer back to full cock. Most of the deer were still grazing, but one was looking right at him with its tail in the air, ready to run. He quickly zeroed in on her and pulled the trigger.

Click!

Orville ducked back behind the fender, beads of sweat lined across his brow. He worked the action forward and back again, ejecting a spent casing as he chambered a fresh round. Lenny's kid should've checked everything before handing him the rifle.

Little twit!

He remounted the hood. The entire herd was looking right at him, startled by the metallic ratcheting of the lever-action rifle.

There was no time. Orville brought the gun to his shoulder and squeezed off a quick round.

The deer suddenly bolted. White tails flagging, they scattered in every direction.

Unsure if he'd hit anything, he quickly stood. He fired round after round into the frantic herd, barely taking time to aim, hoping to take one down, even by luck if need be. His last shot was directed at the bounding rump of a distant deer.

He aimed high. Pulled a quick trigger.

KAPOW!

A flinch? He thought he saw it flinch! A lucky shot to be sure, if he was right. His heart raced. Pounding with excitement.

Oh, how he loved the thrill of the hunt!

The deer had scattered, only to disappear like ghosts. And since Orville was in no condition to walk, Lenny hoofed into the woods and scouted around. He had hoped to come across a blood trail, but when he couldn't find a trace of red anywhere, he hustled back to the truck. After all, it was private property. And inside the house, some big dogs were barking up a storm.

Lenny climbed back inside Orville's truck and slammed the door. "Let's get out of here," he said. "We'll try someplace else; there's still plenty of daylight left."

Orville dropped his truck into gear and started down the road. "Hey kid," he grunted, eyes locked straight ahead. "Next time, make sure I have a live round in the chamber and the safety is off, okay?"

Young Sammy Chunk stared through the windshield in stony silence. His father, seeing he was upset, nudged him with an easy elbow. "Aw, don't let him bother you, son. Everybody screws up once in a while. Ain't that right, Orvy?"

Orrville glanced over at him and snorted. "Humph!"

"Hey, cut the kid a break, will ya? It's his first day out with us."

"But I would've had one, Skinny!"

"Not the way *you* were shooting!"

Orville stepped on the accelerator and began to speed up. Lenny was right, he was never much of a marksman. And now, with the Big C growing inside him, his eyes weren't so good anymore, either.

The second time around, they approached from a westerly direction so the field would be on the driver's side. After road hunting for hours without any luck, Lenny had wanted to return to same spot. And when they did, they saw a small herd of deer grazing in the field, just like before.

"How did you know they'd be back?" asked an astonished Orville.

"Years of experience," replied Lenny with a self-satisfied smile. (He didn't tell Orville about the salt blocks and bushels of apples he'd seen scattered in the field when he went searching for Orville's deer earlier. It was a good bet, he knew, that at least some of the deer would return. Still, even Lenny was surprised to see so many animals.) He nudged his boy. "Daddy's gonna show you how it's done, son. Time to lock and load."

Sammy worked the lever-action Marlin, transporting a fresh round into the chamber as Orville brought his truck to a gradual stop. Lenny took the rifle from his son and eased open the passenger door barely enough to squeeze out.

He hunkered low, creeping along the fender so the deer wouldn't see him. Still spooked from Orville's wild shooting, they'd moved farther away from the road.

And they were more alert.

The entire herd stood woodenly. Ears erect, tails held high as Lenny crouched by the front wheel, hugging his rifle, preparing to stand and shoot. There would be no time to lean across the hood for support. No time to snuggle the rifle into his shoulder for careful aim. He'd have to be fast. The deer were about to explode.

All at once, Lenny sprang to his feet and pointed the rifle at a large doe standing broadside to him. He fired quickly.

Too quickly. A clean miss.

The entire herd bolted in a wild, zigzag pattern, racing toward the neighboring woods. He snapped off two rounds toward the back of the herd. A doe momentarily dropped its haunches, then caught itself and kept running. He watched it disappear into the trees, certain he'd made a lethal hit.

There would be blood in the grass. A trail of it.

All he need do was sit back now. Give the deer a little time to die.

He opened the passenger door and slipped back inside. Handing his son the gun, he looked at Orville. "We'll come back in an hour," he said. "Then you can drop me and Sammy off down the road a ways, out of sight of the house. We'll go in and track it."

Lenny put a long arm around his boy and squeezed him close. "I'm gonna let you gut her, too, son. About time you got a little blood on your hands."

Shirley Smith was driving home with a week's worth of groceries when she crested the hill behind their truck, a short distance away.

Helpless, she watched in horror as Lenny shot at the deer in her yard and then jumped back into Orville's pickup.

Her heart pounding with emotion, she stepped on the accelerator and raced ahead, bringing her vehicle to a grinding halt alongside them.

Three stunned occupants turned at once to gape at her. Her eyes were wounding arrows. She rolled down her window and motioned for Lenny to do likewise.

Orville put his truck in gear, about to speed off, when Lenny snapped his head toward him. "Wait!" he growled urgently. "We don't know what she saw. Maybe I can talk us out of this." He cranked down his window and nodded at her, his face knotted in painful expectation.

"What do you think you're doing?" she cried. "That's my house! I feed those deer all winter long!"

Lenny swallowed hard and managed to eke out a lame smile. "I didn't see no posters saying it was private property, ma'am. It's deer season! Didn't mean to get anybody riled."

"Oh, believe me," she warned, "*riled* doesn't begin to explain how I feel right now. Just because you bought a hunting license, it doesn't give you the right to shoot wherever you happen to see a deer!"

Lenny didn't take well to criticism, and he especially disliked being scolded by a woman. "Whoa, now honey," he said. "Calm down a minute!"

"Don't you dare tell me to calm down, you . . . you . . . Neanderthal!"

Lenny had no idea what a Neanderthal was, but he knew it wasn't good. "Look here, lady," he said, "you got no right to go accusing me of shooting deer on your property!"

"It's not an accusation!" Her tone was acid. "I saw you!"

Lenny rubbed the back of his neck and turned to Orville. "Get ready to roll," he hissed. Looking back at the woman, through gritted teeth he said, "Lady, I got two witnesses sitting right next to me that'll say I never fired a shot. Now, why don't you go into that nice, cozy house over there and bake a pie for your old man."

She was taken aback for a moment, astounded by his arrogance. She quickly shook it off, her eyes boring into him, voice low and scorching. "Mister," she said, reaching into her glove box, "you better get out of here and slink back into the dank cave you came from, while you still can."

Thinking she was going for a gun, Lenny turned white. "Go-go-go!" He barked.

Orville stood on the gas peddle and took off, his tires shooting a spray of road gravel into the front of her car.

Shirley Smith retrieved the cell phone from her glove box, flipped it open, and dialed nine-one-one.

Deputy Jeff Pierce found the suspect's truck parked along the berm within a mile of her home. He'd been patrolling nearby when a dispatcher contacted him about unlawful road hunting in the area. The complainant, Shirley Smith, had provided a vehicle tag number that came back to Orville Odenbock. Pierce had no idea that Lenny Chunk or his son was involved when he pulled up behind them.

As Pierce walked cautiously toward the pickup truck, he recognized Lenny staring out the back window at him. He could see two other passengers inside, and knowing Lenny Chunk was a pathological liar, decided to approach on the opposite side, visually inspecting the pickup's rear for blood or hair as he passed.

Orville cranked his neck over a shoulder. "Afternoon, officer," he said, squinting into the sun. "We haven't even got started yet. Just discussing where we might find some deer. Any suggestions?"

Pierce raised a curious brow. "Suggestions?" he mocked. "Here's one: How about telling me the truth? Your truck was involved in a hunting violation less than an hour ago."

Orville shook his head viciously. "No way! We know just who you're talking about, though. That woman is crazy! All we were doing was looking at the deer. Nobody fired any shots. Honest!"

Pierce expected as much. "How many firearms are in this truck, including handguns?" he asked.

"Just the one thirty-thirty that Sammy's holding. He's Lenny's son. Gun's empty, too. Go ahead and check it if you want."

Pierce saw a half-dozen bullets scattered on the floor. The Marlin's action was open, indicating it had been hastily unloaded seconds before he reached them. The kid was trembling in his seat. He looked like he wanted to puke.

"How old are you, son?" asked Pierce.

Lenny answered for him. "He's twelve, warden. Took him out of school so he could go hunting with me. He's hoping to get his first deer today."

What could be more important than spending quality time with your son? thought Pierce. "Hand the rifle out the window to me," he said. "Butt first."

Orville took the rifle from the boy and passed it out his window. Pierce took it from him and put the muzzle under his nose. It had been recently fired.

Lenny leaned past his son to stare up at Pierce. "Me and the boy was doing a little target shooting this morning," he assured him. "It was on our own property, and we had hay bails for a backstop."

Pierce nodded. "I want you to pick those bullets off the floor and hand them to me."

Lenny reached down and scooped them up. Then he passed the shells to Orville who dropped them into the deputy's hand.

One by one, Pierce ordered each suspect out of the truck and requested to see their identification and hunting licenses. Orville and Sammy both had proper documents but Lenny had nothing. Because he had blundered into them on the way to the complainant's house, Pierce couldn't dispute their claim that they hadn't been hunting. He was anxious to speak with the woman.

"You're all free to leave," he said. "But I'll be holding onto the rifle until my investigation is over."

Orville balked. "That's my gun!" he whined. "You can't just take it like that!"

"It's evidence," said Pierce.

"But that ain't right!"

"I'll give you a receipt."

"A receipt?" scoffed Orville. "You can't hunt with a receipt!"

"That's right," said Pierce.

He drove directly to the house and parked along the road at the edge of the property. Pierce had seen the empty casings even before he exited his vehicle. The bright afternoon sun reflecting off each metal shell. There were eight, in total. All thirty-thirty Winchester. Pierce picked them up with a gloved hand and dropped the brass casings into an evidence envelope.

"Officer!" came a high-pitched voice from behind. "Hello!"

He turned to see a woman in her mid-forties standing by her front door, waving. He walked across the lawn and introduced himself.

"Thank you for coming, officer," she said. "I'm Mrs. Smith—the one who called you."

"I understand you caught some people road hunting here, is that correct?"

"There were three of them," she said. "Two men and a boy. Oh, I think it's terrible to bring up a child that way. What kind of an example is it for a father to show his son?"

"Yes, ma'am."

She briefed him on what had taken place. Then pointed and said, "I walked into the field over there. I found blood from where they shot one of my deer." She shook her head sadly, her face creased with despair. "Do you think it's suffering?"

"I don't know, ma'am. I intend to track it when we're done talking. First, I need to ask you a few questions: Can you identify the men?"

"The skinny one for sure," she said. "The boy too. But you're not going to arrest him . . . please tell me you're not."

"Depends," he said. "What about the driver? Did you get a look at him?"

"I saw his face for a moment. He tried to keep it turned away while I was confronting the other one. But I'd recognize him if I saw him again. He was in his fifties and puffy looking. Dough-faced, like maybe he was sick."

Pierce nodded. It was Odenbock, all right.

"I didn't mention this when I called your agency," she added, "but my teenage daughter stayed home with a bad cold today. They were here earlier this morning as well. She saw them from her bedroom window. The other man, the puffy one, he was shooting at the deer too."

Pierce was surprised to learn this. The fact that he might be able to nail both Lenny and Orville with poaching convictions made his pulse quicken. "We've been after these people for years," he said. "Just can't get anybody to testify against them. Everyone's afraid. Hate to say it, but I may not have much of a case unless you'd be willing to go to court and tell a judge what you saw."

The woman looked at her hands as if counting fingers. "To tell you the truth, officer, I'm afraid too. I live here alone with my daughter, Suzie."

Pierce had expected this. Although disappointed, he couldn't blame her. "I understand," he said. "Call us if you see them in the area again."

She looked up. Her eyes level with his. "I'm afraid, officer, but I won't let that stop me from doing what I must. You go ahead and file your charges. Just promise me something . . ."

"What?"

"That you won't arrest the boy."

"You have a deal."

"Oh—and there's one more thing . . ."

"Ma'am?"

"Promise me that you'll prosecute those two wicked men for every single violation you can think of."

Pierce smiled. "Word of honor."

Pierce followed the blood trail into the woods for only a hundred yards when he came to the carcass. A single bullet had brought her down. Shot in the neck, the doe had bled to death quickly.

The bullet passed straight though, leaving no chance for a ballistics analysis proving Orville's thirty-thirty had killed the deer. This would make testimony from an eyewitness crucial. Although ballistics would inevitably match the empty casings along the road with the Marlin he'd seized, it wouldn't prove who pulled the trigger. Pierce needed eyewitness testimony to connect Lenny to the deer he'd found.

Convinced he could win the case in court, Pierce filed citations against Lenny Chunk for hunting without orange clothing, hunting without a license, failure to produce identification, hunting in a safety zone, using a vehicle to hunt, shooting across a roadway, and attempting to kill more than one doe in a season. Orville Odenbock was charged with road hunting and a safety zone violation.

Lenny took a hearing and was found guilty of all charges after the judge heard testimony from Shirley Smith and her daughter. He was sentenced to pay two-thousand dollars in fines and had his hunting license revoked for three years. Orville Odenbock never took a hearing but pled guilty to his charges. He passed away a short time later.

Sammy Chunk, as promised, was not prosecuted for any game law violations. The following year, however, he was caught smoking pot after school. His father hated dope smokers and was mortified when the police brought Sammy home. He told his son that he'd embarrassed the entire family—cousins, uncles, aunts, grandparents—everyone! Word gets around, his father wailed. They're all going to hear about this!

Sammy started bawling. Then he looked his father in the eye, tears streaming down flushed cheeks, and asked why it was okay for him to choose the laws that *he* wanted to break but not for his son do the same.

"Don't you see? I'm no different than you, Dad," he said through his sobs. "Your son is just like you."

Acknowledgements

I would like to thank my beautiful wife, Mary Ann, for the endless hours she endured listening to me babble on about the different stories in this book, and for her encouragement and help in bringing my manuscript to fruition.

Thanks to my twin brother, John, for artfully designing my book cover and for the cougar photograph in the story *Footsteps in the Dark*. View John's photos:
www.johnwasserman.com

Thanks to David Larnerd for the outstanding wildlife photographs used inside this book. View Dave's photos:
www.pbase.com/yellowdogdave

Thanks to Timothy Flanigan for the beautiful cover photograph of a bald eagle in flight. View Dave's photos:
www.natureexposure.com

Thanks to Deputy Gene Gaydos and Deputy Jeff Pierce for your friendship and your untiring dedication to our wildlife resources. You were always there when I needed you.

About the Author

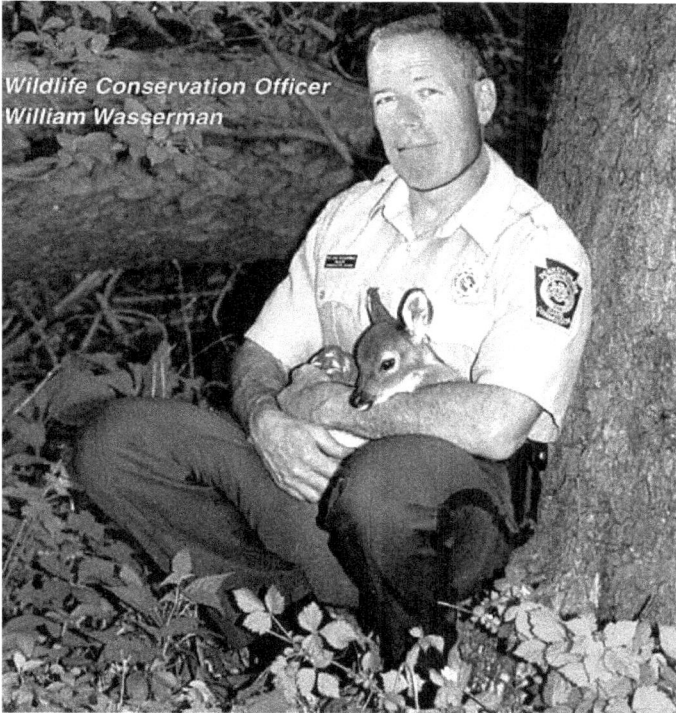

Wildlife Conservation Officer
William Wasserman

William Wasserman started his career with the Pennsylvania Game Commission in 1974 and retired after thirty-two years of dedicated service. Wasserman is a prolific writer who has been published in dozens of national magazines including *Black Belt, Fur-Fish-Game, Pennsylvania Game News, International Game Warden, South Carolina Wildlife,* and *The Alberta Game Warden.* He also penned a weekly outdoor newspaper column for fifteen years and hosted a popular outdoor talk-radio program for eight years. He has written six books about his life as a state game warden.